Equal Justice

A Biography of

Sandra Day O'Connor

Harold and Geraldine Woods

REACHING OUT
BOOKS

Dillon Press, Inc.
Minneapolis, Minnesota 55415

The authors would like to thank Justice O'Connor for her cooperation and kindness. In addition, we are grateful to John O'Connor, Mr. and Mrs. Harry Day, Senator Barry Goldwater, John P. Frank, and Carolyn Warner, who provided us with anecdotes, comments, and photos for inclusion in this book.

Photographs courtesy of the following:

> AP/Wide World—76, 77, 83
> The Day Family/Lazy B Cattle Company—26, 27, 28, 29, 30, 31
> Larry Downing/Newsweek—80
> Michael Evans/The White House—79
> Mary Ann Fackelman/The White House—back cover
> Bruce Hoertel/Newsweek—82, front cover
> Phoenix Newspapers, Inc.—32, 33
> Stanford University—6
> © The Supreme Court Historical Society—81
> UPI—76

Library of Congress Cataloging in Publication Data

Woods, Harold.
Equal justice: a biography of Sandra Day O'Connor.

Bibliography: p.
Includes index.
SUMMARY: A biography of Sandra Day O'Connor, the first woman Supreme Court justice, which includes her childhood, her early legal career, and her life since her appointment.
  1. O'Connor, Sandra Day, 1930-   —Juvenile literature.
2. Judges—United States—Biography   —Juvenile literature.
[1. O'Connor, Sandra Day, 1930-   2. Judges.   3. United States. Supreme Court—Biography] I. Woods, Geraldine.   II. Title.
KF8745.025W66   1985347.73'2634 [B]   84-23042
ISBN 0-87518-292-5   347.3073534 [B]   [92]

© 1985 by Dillon Press, Inc. All rights reserved

Dillon Press, Inc., 242 Portland Avenue South
Minneapolis, Minnesota 55415

Printed in the United States of America

   2   3   4   5   6   7   8   9   10 91 90 89 88 87 86

Contents

Introduction	"It belongs to man to make, apply, and execute the law."	4
Chapter One	"It is very different from growing up in a city."	7
Chapter Two	"Many women are happier juggling the various roles than not having the opportunity. I'm like that."	19
Chapter Three	"I ended up being the majority leader."	34
Chapter Four	". . .A marvelous experience with a new branch of government."	42
Chapter Five	"I did not know whether. . . I should accept it if I was offered the chance."	51
Chapter Six	"Here Lies a Good Judge"	60
Chapter Seven	". . .To administer justice without respect to persons and with equal rights to the poor and the rich."	70
Chapter Eight	". . .A total commitment to the work."	84
Chapter Nine	"History will have to determine that."	95
Postscript		106
Appendix One	Other Members of the Supreme Court	110
Appendix Two	Famous Supreme Court Cases	117
Bibliography		123
Index		125

Introduction

"It belongs to man to make, apply, and execute the law."

In 1873, it was against the law in the state of Illinois for a woman to become a lawyer. When the law was challenged in the Supreme Court, the Court's decision was clear:

> Man is, or should be, woman's protector and defender. The natural and proper timidity and delicacy which belongs to the female sex evidently unfits it for many of the occupations of civil life. The constitution [makeup] of the family organization, which is founded in the divine ordinance [by God] as well as in the nature of things, indicates the domestic sphere [the home] as that which properly belongs to the domain and functions of womanhood.

In the same case, *Bradwell* v. *Illinois*, the Court went on to say that "God designated the sexes to occupy different spheres of action. It belongs to man to make, apply, and execute the law."

On September 25, 1981, a woman named Sandra Day O'Connor stood in the same building where that decision was written. Not only was she a lawyer; she had been a state senator and a judge. She had, in the words of the 1873 Supreme Court decision, "made, applied, and executed the law." As President Ronald Reagan watched, Mrs. O'Connor raised her hand and swore to uphold the laws of the United States. In just under a minute, she became a justice of the Supreme Court, the highest court in our country. She was the first woman ever to hold that position.

It took two hundred years for the barrier against women to fall at the Supreme Court, but then, barriers fall slowly there. In 1790 George Washington named the first six justices. Every single one of them was male, white, and a member of the Protestant faith. For almost fifty years, every member of the Court fit that description. Then, in 1836, President Andrew Jackson broke tradition by appointing Roger Taney. Taney, although white and male, was a Roman Catholic. Eighty years later, in 1916, President Woodrow Wilson selected the first Jewish justice, Louis Brandeis, for the Supreme Court. Over a hundred years after Washington made his appointments to the Court, a non-white finally sat on the Bench. Thurgood Marshall, nominated by President Lyndon Johnson in 1967, was the first black man to be a justice of the Supreme Court.

Justice Marshall's appointment was a great breakthrough, but there was still one last barrier that hadn't fallen. It was up to Sandra Day O'Connor to help it fall—a pioneer's job, but then, she had come from a pioneering family.

Chapter/One

"It is very different from growing up in a city."

Quite a few years ago, some missionaries explained heaven to a group of American Indians who lived in the Arizona desert. To their amazement, the Indians told them that they didn't want to go to heaven when they died. To them, Arizona seemed much nicer than the paradise the missionaries described!

Southeastern Arizona seems anything but heaven. It is harsh and sun-baked. There is little water; less than ten inches of rain falls there in an average year. Many scientists consider the region a splendid laboratory for studying how plants adapt to an unfriendly environment. Yet southeastern Arizona is also a place of great beauty. The air is fresh and clear, and the sky and land seem to be colored with extra intensity.

Paradise or not, southeastern Arizona is a sharp contrast to the rolling green hills of Vermont, where Sandra Day O'Connor's ancestors once lived. About a hundred years ago—thirty years before Arizona was admitted to the Union—Sandra's grandfather, Henry Clay Day, became one in a tide of people traveling west in search of a better life. Day first settled in Wichita, Kansas, where he prospered in real estate and lumber. He and Alice, his wife, then became true pioneers, staking out 155,000 acres of land that became the Lazy B ranch. The Lazy B is located between Lordsburg, New Mexico and Duncan, Arizona. Henry Clay Day's cattle ranch was, according to one old newspaper, the first ranch in southeastern Arizona.

Sandra's father, Harry Day, grew up on the Lazy B, and inherited and ran the ranch when his father died. Harry Day needed a strong dose of his father's pioneer spirit to keep the Lazy B running. When Henry Clay Day had died, the family was living in Pasadena, California, where Harry had attended high school. The man who was running the ranch in their absence did not do well, and the ranch was not making any money. Also, in times of drought there was not enough water to keep the herds alive. During the Great Depression of the 1930s, the Lazy B was hard hit by a number of dry years. Once, Harry Day had little more than five hundred dollars left to his name. He recalls that at his lowest point, someone offered him a cent and a half per pound for his cows. However, the cows were in such bad shape that the agreement fell through! Finally, President Franklin D. Roosevelt's New Deal programs bailed out ranchers: the government paid them twelve dollars a head for sickly cows and even more for healthy ones. With that help, the Lazy B was saved.

Sandra's mother, Ada Mae Wilkey, had lived in Duncan, Arizona, near the Lazy B, for much of her childhood. When Ada Mae was ready to go to school, her parents moved to El Paso, Texas, where her father carved out a career as a merchant and a banker. Ada Mae's life in El Paso was quite different from the future that awaited her at the Lazy B. El Paso, a thriving city, provided Ada Mae with many cultural and educational experiences. She even toured Europe with her classmates when she was sixteen years old. After high school, Ada Mae entered and eventually graduated from the University of Arizona. She did this at a time when few women went on to college—proof that she matched her future husband in pioneer spirit. Ada Mae met Harry Day a short while after her graduation. After their marriage, the couple settled at the Lazy B. When asked if it was difficult to give up city life in El Paso for the isolation of the ranch, Ada Mae said no. "I just loved Harry so much," she later told a reporter.

In those days, the Lazy B was definitely not a luxury estate. The ranch had only a simple, four-room house without indoor plumbing, running water, or electricity. Even the radio was unreliable—it would not work when there was a sudden change in temperature. Still, the Lazy B was one of the first ranches in the country to utilize solar energy. Harry Day read about the then-new inventions in a pamphlet from the University of California, and built his own solar heaters. They are still in use today on the Lazy B.

About three years after her marriage, Ada Mae became pregnant with her first child. She went to El Paso to stay with her mother, since there were no doctors near the Lazy B. Ada Mae gave birth to a baby girl there on March 26, 1930, and named the child

Sandra. On the day of Sandra's birth, perhaps as an omen of her future career, Harry Day was in court in Tucson, Arizona. He was in the middle of a complicated legal case involving the Lazy B. (The case would continue until his infant daughter's tenth birthday.) With characteristic humor, Harry Day later told an interviewer that, though he had never urged Sandra to become a lawyer, his long legal battle made him wish for some legal advice somewhere in his family!

While Sandra was still an infant, her mother brought her back to the family ranch. She lived there until it was time for her to attend kindergarten; after that she went away to school and was there only during the summer and other long vacations. Still, Sandra recalls the part of her childhood she spent on the ranch with great affection. Her face glows as she describes the desert animals she once adopted as pets: "On a ranch, you get to see every kind of animal at close range. As I grew up we had a pet bobcat [that] stayed in the house. He was a huge animal. When he purred you could hear it all over the house! We also had a family of skunks that lived under the old screened porch. We had wild javelina hogs, a desert terrapin; we even had a porcupine once. We also had pet goats and a raccoon—just all kinds of animals!"

Though she loved animals, Sandra also saw them with a rancher's eye. Her father expected everyone who lived on the Lazy B to help keep the "critter" population low. This meant that any animals that could harm the Lazy B herd—either directly, or indirectly by eating some of the scarce vegetation—were supposed to be killed. Sandra became an excellent shot

with a twenty-two caliber rifle, and hunted jack rabbits, prairie dogs, coyotes, rattlesnakes, and Gila mon-
sters (poisonous desert lizards).

Sandra picked up other unusual skills while she
was growing up. As she says, "It is very different from
growing up in a city. When you grow up on a ranch,
you tend to participate along with everyone else in
whatever the activity is that's going on around you. If
there's a roundup, then everyone gets involved in working on the roundup. If there's a fence to be fixed, or if
there's a gate . . . or a well to be repaired, then every-
body participates." Sandra joined her father's ranch
hands in these activities. As part of her work on the
ranch, she also learned to drive when she was only
seven years old! By the time she was ten, Sandra could
handle a tractor or a truck with ease. (A license is not
required to drive a car on private land.) As her cousin,
Flournoy Manzo, said to one interviewer, "We knew
what to do with screwdrivers and nails . . . living on a
ranch made us very self-sufficient."

At least one member of the family had some
doubts about Sandra's unusual childhood experiences.
While Sandra was attending school, she lived with her
grandmother. Mrs. Wilkey once scolded Harry Day
for letting Sandra ride in the rumble seat of a car while
perched on top of a box of dynamite that was needed
for the ranch! Flournoy recalls that Grandmother Wilkey occasionally swatted Flournoy and Sandra with a
yardstick when they got into mischief.

Sandra also enjoyed some traditionally female
activities: Ada Mae Day, a great cook, taught her skills
to her daughter; Sandra played with dolls with her

cousin Flournoy; and both enjoyed games. The two girls swam in the large tanks of water on the ranch, and fished in them with strings and safety pins.

Reading also absorbed much of their time. Harry Day had a fairly good collection of books, and ordered new ones almost every month by mail. As Sandra says, "Reading was one of my main avocations [hobbies] as I grew up. At the ranch, my parents luckily enjoyed having a lot of books around, and we had a rather extensive library compared to most of the families that I knew. I simply spent a lot of time reading, whether it was magazine articles, or books, or whatever." Flournoy recalls that the two girls read everything they could get their hands on, including the *Los Angeles Times*, the *Wall Street Journal, National Geographic* magazine, and other periodicals. At times, the girls read aloud to each other from the *Saturday Evening Post*.

Another favorite pastime was riding. "I had several horses of my own while I was growing up," says Sandra O'Connor. She continues to ride as an adult. Her brother Alan once told an interviewer that even after Sandra became a judge she often joined the family at roundup time. He says she was just an average rider, though she became "kind of sore" since she wasn't riding regularly! He believes that she enjoyed "being with the family and hanging around cowboys, riding in the hills and watching the sunsets."

The time she spent on the ranch helped knit the closeness Sandra enjoyed with her family. As she says, "My father was in and out of the house all day long. It wasn't a job where the father goes off and works during the day and comes back at five o'clock. It goes on around the clock and everyone is involved." The Day family always sat together for every meal, and provided companionship for each other. Besides Flournoy and her brother Alan, who today manages the Lazy B, Sandra also played with her sister Ann. There were cowboys living on the Lazy B when Sandra was a child; roundup cook Bug Quinn and cowboy Claude Tibbets paid a lot of attention to the little girl. Sandra says, "You tend not to have children your own age available to be with you [when you grow up on a ranch]. My earliest companions, aside from my parents, were the cowboys on the ranch."

The distance of the ranch from "civilization" was the main reason Sandra was sent to El Paso, Texas when she was old enough to start school. Harry and Ada Mae Day realized that their daughter was an extremely bright child. They wanted to give her an education that would stimulate her growing mind. Unfortunately, there were no excellent schools close to the ranch. As Sandra says, "The roads weren't all that good. Even automobiles were not that good, and it was too far to try to drive." So at the age of five Sandra went to live with her grandmother. She attended the Radford School, a private school for girls in a quiet section of the city.

Although Sandra enjoyed her school days, she missed the carefree life of the ranch. Today she says with feeling, "I was very, very homesick whenever I was not at the ranch." She often invited school friends to the Lazy B during holidays. At the end of many visits to the ranch, Sandra would be reluctant to leave for Texas. Sometimes, the little girl hid herself in a pile of hay, hoping to avoid the trip. Occasionally, the trip back to El Paso was delayed because of the weather. No one seemed to mind spending a few extra days on the ranch, waiting out a storm.

While at Radford, Sandra was an excellent student. She now says, "I suppose that I enjoyed history classes and English classes, and I know that I enjoyed Spanish classes very much. I think those were probably my favorites." (Later, in another school where most of the students were Spanish speaking, Sandra made the highest grades in her language courses. Years after, when she was a judge on the Arizona Court of Appeals, Sandra O'Connor's license plate read "Jueza," which means "woman judge" in Spanish.) She admired several of her teachers, especially her junior high history and civics instructor, as well as the dramatic arts teacher. "I learned from her how to give a talk, be in a play, and make other public appearances. She was an excellent teacher," said Sandra O'Connor. Certainly all those skills would come in handy in her later career!

As Sandra grew older, the Day family often traveled together during school vacations. During years of sufficient rainfall, when there was plenty of grass for the livestock and a higher income for the family, the Days often attended cattle ranchers' conventions in various Western cities. One year they set out to visit every state capital west of the Mississippi River. On another occasion the Days went to Honduras and Cuba. (Cuba was quite popular with American tourists before the communist revolution.) The family traveled to those places on a banana boat! Sandra also made frequent trips to California with her parents.

By the time she was thirteen, Sandra very much wanted to come home to the Lazy B. She transferred to a school in Lordsburg, New Mexico. Though it was her "local" school, it was twenty-two long miles from the ranch. Sandra had to be driven to a neighbor's house to meet the school bus before dawn each day. She didn't return to the Lazy B until after sunset. This difficult daily journey may have helped form Sandra's attitude towards school busing, a method of desegregation that is often used to create racial balance in schools. During the Senate confirmation hearing held when she was a candidate for the Supreme Court, the future justice was asked for her opinion on this much-discussed topic. Perhaps thinking of her own experience, she replied that "the transportation of students over long distances can be a very disruptive part of any child's educational background."

After a year in Lordsburg, Sandra could no longer handle the long hours of traveling. She returned to Radford for a year, and then attended Austin High School in El Paso. Her friends noted that during her year at home, Sandra had matured. She had gone back to the Lazy B as a child, but returned to El Paso as a tall, slim, elegant young woman. In fact, many of her classmates considered her very mature for her age, if rather shy. Sandra achieved excellent grades, and was placed in the school's honor classes. She was interested in more than her studies, however. Like most high school girls she had "crushes" from time to time, and enjoyed discussing boys with her friends.

Sandra was so bright that she easily earned the

required number of credits for her high school diploma a year ahead of the normal age. Though she was only sixteen when she graduated from high school, she was admitted to Stanford University in California, a famous school that accepts only a small fraction of the students who apply there. Sandra's father, Harry Day, had once planned on attending Stanford, but Harry had to abandon his plans when his father died and left the Lazy B in his care. When he gave up his own dream for a college education, however, Harry Day vowed to provide better opportunities for his children. Sandra was so sure that she wanted to attend Stanford, her father's favorite school, that she didn't even bother to apply to any other colleges. Her academic record was excellent, so she was immediately accepted.

Though she had lived in El Paso for a number of years and traveled all over with her family, Sandra had still lived a fairly protected life before going to Stanford. When she first arrived there, her father had to show her how to write out a check! Once at the university, however, the young college student quickly settled in and began to distinguish herself in her classes. Her sophomore roommate, Marilyn Schwartz Brown, remembers Sandra as a "very shy girl." She once described the future Supreme Court justice to an interviewer: "Even though she was younger than us," recalled Marilyn, "she always seemed to handle it [school]. She never got upset. She never went into a panic about anything. She was easy to get along with and she was fun."

Sandra majored in economics while at Stanford, though she was unsure of her future plans. At that point she had never considered law as a career. For a while, she thought she might own and manage a ranch of her own someday or run the Lazy B with her family. Her ties to her home were still very strong. She often brought groups of friends home to Arizona for every roundup, as she had during her high school years.

By 1949, after only three years in college, Sandra had completed most of the requirements for her degree. While finishing her senior year, she took some courses at Stanford Law School. To her surprise, she was fascinated with this new area of study. So in 1950, when her undergraduate work was completed, Sandra entered Stanford Law School as a full-time student. Again, Stanford Law School is so good that many people consider it an honor even to gain admittance there—and Sandra was a full three years younger than most of her classmates!

Sandra dug into her legal studies with her usual enthusiasm. She earned membership in the Order of the Coif, an honor society, and was appointed to the board of editors of the *Stanford Law Review*, a magazine of articles on legal affairs. These honors are only awarded to the best students from each class.

Sandra's work on the law journal had an unexpected fringe benefit. John Jay O'Connor III, the son of a San Francisco doctor and a student in the class behind Sandra's, was also a member of the staff of the *Stanford Law Review*. One day, John and Sandra were assigned to the same article. Apparently, it was love at first sight. As John O'Connor says now, "My wife and I met at Stanford Law School. We had not met each other there until we were given a joint assignment on the *Stanford Law Review*. Our job was to check the citations [list of quoted material] in an article written by someone else and to proofread the galley proof of the article. We had to do the citation checking in the library. As we did this, we talked a lot, and my wife-to-be would laugh and laugh as I told her funny stories or made funny comments. After we finished checking the citations, I suggested that we could do the proofreading somewhere else. We went to a local restaurant, quickly did the proofreading, and then just began to talk. We liked each other immediately. We went out the next two or three nights, and then one night I asked for dates for the next five nights. She agreed. We ended up going out the next forty-two nights in a row! Neither one of us went out with another person after we met each other."

In 1952, Sandra graduated from law school. She had finished her bachelor's degree and her Doctor of Law degree in only six years—a course that normally takes seven. She graduated third in a class of one hundred and two students. (William Rehnquist, a friend who is also a Supreme Court justice, was first in the same class.) A year later, John O'Connor graduated and the couple married. The wedding took place on Sandra's beloved Lazy B, in the living room of the ranch house. The reception was held in a new barn that had recently been built on the property. Sandra's childhood and school years were over; it was time to begin her marriage and career.

Chapter/Two

/ "Many women are
happier juggling the
various roles than not
having the opportunity.
I'm like that."

After finishing law school, Sandra Day O'Connor
went searching for a job. She had graduated from
Stanford with high honors, so quite reasonably, the
new Mrs. O'Connor expected that she would be hired
by an important private law firm. However, there was
one, major "drawback"—she was a woman. She went
from law firm to law firm in several California cities
with her impressive records in hand, and she was told
over and over again that there weren't any openings for
her. "I interviewed with law firms in Los Angeles and
San Francisco, but none had ever hired a woman as a
lawyer before, and they were not prepared to do so,"
explains Justice O'Connor.

One of the firms at which she was interviewed was
Gibson, Dunn, and Crutcher. After reviewing her qualifications, they offered Sandra O'Connor a position as
a legal secretary. A legal secretary is a secretary who
knows something about law terms. It is a higher

position than that of a general secretary, but it is much lower than that of a lawyer. This was their offer to a person who had graduated third in her class at Stanford Law School! (One of the partners in Gibson, Dunn, and Crutcher in later years was William French Smith. Almost thirty years after this job offer was made, William French Smith called Sandra O'Connor at her home in Paradise Valley, Arizona. He was then the attorney general of the United States. He represented President Ronald Reagan, and was talking about a slightly better offer to Judge O'Connor—a seat on the Supreme Court!)

It was a discouraging time for the new lawyer, but Sandra Day O'Connor has never given up easily. Since no private firm seemed to want her, she accepted a job as deputy attorney of San Mateo County, California. When Justice O'Connor speaks of that time in her life, she is not bitter. On the contrary, she is thankful that events led her to work for the government. "I was happy to get that job," she says. "It was in the public sector, where opportunities for women were better at the time, better than the private sector. It turned out to be a very happy choice for me because I remained in the public sector for most of my life." Though she does not hold a grudge, she did comment once to a reporter, "Women have to perform better than their male counterparts to succeed in competition."

As county deputy attorney, Sandra O'Connor represented San Mateo whenever it was involved in a lawsuit. "I worked primarily on the civil [non-criminal] side," she says, "advising different county agencies and boards and institutions . . . a fire department, a police department or a school district or a flood control district, things of that kind."

John and Sandra O'Connor only stayed in San Mateo for a year because John was soon drafted and sent to West Germany by the army. He worked with the Judge Advocate's department as an army lawyer. Sandra got a job with the army, too. She worked for three years as a civilian lawyer for the United States Forces in Frankfurt. Mrs. O'Connor worked mainly with contracts, helping the American government buy and sell supplies on the international market.

When the O'Connors arrived in Germany, World War II had been over for only a short time. The German people were just beginning to recover from the destruction to their country caused by the war and the Nazi government. In another couple of years, people would refer to the German recovery as a "miracle," but while the O'Connors were there, the miracle had not yet happened. Certain consumer goods such as clothes and shoes were still in short supply, and rubble from buildings which had been bombed ten years before was not an uncommon sight.

The newlyweds enjoyed the experience of being in Europe at such a historic time. As Sandra O'Connor says, "It was a wonderful time to be there because the early hardships of the postwar years were beginning to be overcome . . . . Some of the . . . tragedy of the war had been put behind the country . . . . We were able to make friends with people in Germany. Many German citizens were willing to be friendly to us."

The O'Connors managed to have a little fun while they were in Europe, too. They visited many European countries during weekends and when John had leave. Sandra and John celebrated the end of his tour of duty with a three-month long holiday of skiing in the mountains of Austria.

In 1957 the couple returned to the United States and settled in Phoenix, Arizona to begin their family and careers in earnest. Sandra was already pregnant with Scott, the first of the three O'Connor sons. After weeks of reviewing their law studies, Sandra and John O'Connor took and passed the Arizona bar exam, which they needed to do to practice law in the state. Almost at the same time, Scott was born.

John O'Connor went to work for a private law firm, and Sandra soon formed a law partnership in a suburb of Phoenix. From their office in a neighborhood shopping center, Lawyer O'Connor and her partner took cases which ranged from writing leases for landlords to defending people accused of drunk driving. They also accepted clients that the courts gave them. These people were too poor to pay for a lawyer, so the court paid lawyers to work for these indigents.

All during this time, Sandra O'Connor had to arrange for babysitters while she kept appointments in her office or at court. Years later, in a speech she gave to the graduates of Columbia College, Justice O'Connor drew on her own experiences as a wife, mother, and career woman. She told an audience of young women, "Most women are able to handle multiple roles exceedingly well.... Women have a great deal of stamina and strength. It is possible to plan both a family and a career and to enjoy success at both.... You [young women] will probably work harder than your spouse to accomplish this, and you will have to become a real efficiency expert, both at home and at work. But you can do it if you choose." At another time, speaking to a reporter, she said, "Many women are happier juggling various roles than not having the opportunity. I'm like that."

Lawyer O'Connor was able to maintain her career for about two years, until her second child, Brian, was born. Three years later the last O'Connor son, Jay, would arrive. Caring for her children was more than a full-time job, so Sandra O'Connor had to drop her law practice. "I found that there was more [work] than I could do—to go to the office every day and take care of the children," she later said. Like many career women, her decision was partly based on her childcare arrangements. "I had a lovely woman who babysat for me with my first child," she said, "but she moved to California and I no longer had her help. It made it impossible at that time to continue my law practice. I was out of the work force as a regular paid employee for about five years, although I did a lot of volunteer work and other activities."

One of Lawyer O'Connor's volunteer activities was working with the Arizona Republican Party. For five years she served as a Republican county precinct committee member. In 1962, she was a Republican district chair. In these positions she participated in the most basic level of our democracy, helping to choose and campaign for candidates for local offices, encouraging people to register and vote, and raising funds for the party. Besides being on the Maricopa Board of Adjustments and Appeals, she served on the

Governor's Committee on Marriage and Family. She also gave time and energy to the Arizona branch of the Salvation Army, and volunteered in a local school, working mainly with black and Hispanic children.

When asked if she enjoyed being a full-time parent, Sandra O'Connor replied, "It was fun, but I missed the workplace and I didn't want to lose touch completely with the work force, so I accepted a lot of jobs that would keep me partially in touch . . . with what was going on." Her activities outside the home also filled her need to be of service to the community.

Typically, Sandra O'Connor threw herself into both career and home with great energy. During this period, she and her husband had a house built for their growing family in a suburb of Phoenix called Paradise Valley. One friend who visited the O'Connors while the house was under construction was surprised to see the couple soaking adobe bricks in milk. Sandra O'Connor explained that the milk bath was an old technique to improve the quality of the bricks. She also told her friend that skim milk was an absolute necessity for the job—homogenized milk didn't work!

Another "volunteer" activity Mrs. O'Connor enjoyed was playing Cupid for her unmarried friends and relatives. She introduced her sister Ann to her future husband, and arranged many other meetings between single people she knew. Friends say that, with typical thoroughness, Mrs. O'Connor was always willing to introduce a friend to several partners until the perfect one was found. Today, she laughingly refers to herself as the yenta (matchmaker) of Paradise Valley.

In 1965, Lawyer O'Connor returned to full-time

work as an assistant attorney general for the state of Arizona. She told a reporter that she wanted to give up being a "compulsive volunteer" and go back to regular work because she felt it would be more relaxing. "When I first started," she says, "I worked as an administrative assistant at the state hospital and did a lot of legal work for them. Then I moved directly into the attorney general's office and had an assignment representing a wide variety of state agencies. I continued to do some work for the hospital but also did work for the welfare department, various boards, commissions, and state offices and agencies."

Lawyer O'Connor enjoyed the variety at the attorney general's office. "I had a wonderful time," she continues. "It was a delightful period in my life. I liked the people with whom I worked very much. We were congenial [friendly] and I learned so much. Part of the pleasure in being in a state attorney general's office is that you have so much responsibility at an early age— much more so than might be true in a private practice where you might have to work many years before you can handle the type of cases that I was able to handle with relatively little experience."

Sandra Day spent her early years on her parents' ranch, but when the bright little girl was old enough for school, Harry and Ada Mae Day sent her to El Paso, Texas, where she lived with her grandmother and attended the Radford School.

On Easter in 1940 Ada Mae holds Sandra's brother Alan while sitting next to Ann and Sandra. Sandra often hid herself when vacations on the ranch ended and she had to leave for school in El Paso.

By the time she had gotten into high school, Sandra had grown tall and slender. Like many high school girls she had crushes and talked about boys, besides being a good student.

Sandra graduated from Austin High School when she was just sixteen. The only college she considered and applied to was Stanford University in California, where she easily won acceptance.

College days were busy, happy times for Sandra. She again got top grades, graduated from college and law school in six (instead of seven) years, and met her future husband, John O'Connor.

Sandra Day O'Connor throughout her life came back to the Lazy B ranch to renew her spirits. She once told President Reagan that she'd rather be "on a good cutting horse working cattle" than doing almost anything else.

John O'Connor enlisted in the army after graduation from law school, and Sandra went with him overseas as a civilian lawyer with the army. Ada Mae and Harry Day came to Germany to visit the young couple.

Senator O'Connor during her term in the Arizona state senate. She was known as a painstaking legislator who voted for or against bills not because of any party position, but because of the merits of each bill.

In the judicial branch of Arizona government, Sandra O'Connor served in the Maricopa County Superior Court system for five years before being appointed to the Arizona Court of Appeals in 1979. Here John O'Connor helps her on with her judge's robe at her swearing in.

Chapter/Three

"I ended up being the majority leader."

In 1969, when Arizona State Senator Isabel A. Burgess accepted a new position in Washington, Governor Jack Williams was responsible for filling her vacant seat in the state legislature with the most qualified person he could find. He chose Sandra Day O'Connor.

The appointment was an important step in Sandra O'Connor's career. During her years as a lawyer and as an assistant attorney general, she had been able to see at first hand how the judicial branch of the government functioned. Therefore, she had a keen understanding of how the law operated in the courtroom. By moving to the legislature, she would be seeing the law from a completely different perspective. There she would be involved in actually writing the laws by which the State of Arizona was governed.

(Her appointment to the legislature was only temporary, however. When Ms. Burgess's term expired, Sandra O'Connor had to campaign for the seat to which she had been appointed. She ran on the Republican ticket and defeated another woman who was the Democratic candidate. After that term Sandra O'Connor ran again and won a second term, and spent a total of five years in the senate.)

The new senator immediately impressed the other legislators by her attention to detail and her determination to do the job well. She was recognized as a natural leader. Right after she had won her first election, and was still relatively inexperienced in her job, the president of the Arizona Senate, William Jacquin, asked her if she would consider running for the post of senate majority leader. The majority leader is the head of whichever party controls the largest number of seats in the senate, and has a great deal of responsibility. Working with other officials, the majority leader chooses legislation that the party considers extremely important. He or she works out how to pass or defeat a particular law. This might include persuading all the senators of the party to vote the same way, convincing the people of the state that the party's position is wise, or negotiating compromises.

Though she knew it was an honor to be singled out for such a position, Senator O'Connor realized that she wasn't yet ready for such responsibility. She told Mr. Jacquin that she declined, explaining, "I've just been elected for the first time, and I've never even been a committee chairman—it wouldn't be fair to the others, and it wouldn't be right—I'm not ready."

She was later appointed chair of the powerful State-County Municipal Affairs Committee where she gained some much-needed experience. Speaking of her first years in the senate, she later said, "I didn't know what the experience in the legislature would be. But I was fortunate in having a very nice set of committee assignments and being chairman of the State-County Municipal Affairs Committee right away. That was great because most of the legislation affecting the state flowed through the committee. Because of my work there, I ended up being the majority leader."

Though she had never seen herself as a champion of feminism, during her five years in the senate Sandra Day O'Connor helped amend laws that discriminated against women. One of the laws she campaigned against said that any property held in common by a husband and wife was under the control of the husband. Under this law's provisions, the woman in a marriage had almost no control of her family's finances. Senator O'Connor used her power in the state legislature to take that law off the books. One Phoenix attorney who helped her on the husband-wife property bill recalls that Senator O'Connor asked a group of senators, business leaders, feminists, and lawyers to advise her while she drafted the legislation. She tapped their talents to make a well-written law, and then used her influence in the senate to get it passed.

Senator O'Connor sponsored bills to make Arizona's youth loans available to girls as well as boys. She was also in favor of the Equal Rights Amendment (ERA), a proposed amendment to the United States Constitution which would prohibit discrimination because of sex. She called for a statewide vote on the amendment in 1974, though she was unsuccessful in this effort. Other legislation encouraged by Senator

O'Connor included a proposal to create a Medicaid system in Arizona. Medicaid is a type of health insurance for poor people, financed by taxes and administered by the state government. Despite Sandra O'Connor's efforts, the bill did not pass, leaving Arizona one of the few states without this type of insurance. Senator O'Connor also voted to bring back the death penalty in her state, and supported a resolution calling on Congress to end forced busing of children to achieve a balance of races in the nation's schools. She also voted for bills to limit government spending, and tried to revise tax laws so that both poor and rich counties in her state would receive equal amounts of state tax money.

Years later, after she had been nominated as associate justice of the Supreme Court, many people would comb through her record in the legislature. They wanted to forecast how she would vote on some of the controversial issues she would be facing if she were on the highest court in the land. These investigators found that her voting record reflected a person who studied each issue on its own merits and then voted for or against it. Though she was majority leader, Senator O'Connor did not go along with the party in every case, as some legislators do. She was loyal to the positions of her party, but more loyal to her own ideals. To Sandra Day O'Connor, the deciding factor was always the worth of each individual piece of legislation.

However, one characteristic of Senator O'Connor which clearly comes across to the observer is her dedication to detail. She was determined to make the laws which emerged from the Arizona state senate as perfectly written as possible. This was important to her; she knew from her years in court that any vagueness would lead to scores of lawsuits.

Sandra O'Connor was known as one of the most painstaking legislators ever. She was so careful that she once offered an amendment to a bill because just a single comma was out of place! She was afraid the faulty punctuation might let the law be misinterpreted.

For a bill to be properly written, a legislator does not just watch the commas. He or she also has to properly research the law and all the effects it might have. In the legislature, this is called "doing your homework." A legislator might be able to give stirring speeches on the merits of a particular bill, but if he or she hasn't done the necessary homework, there is a good chance of losing any debate which might follow a bill's proposal in the legislature.

Senator O'Connor had a reputation as someone who always walked into a debate well prepared. She knew her subject so thoroughly that she almost always overpowered her opponents. A Democratic state senator, a member of the opposing party during Sandra O'Connor's years in the legislature, recalled to an interviewer, "It was impossible to win a debate with her. We'd [the Democrats] go on to the floor with a few facts and let rhetoric do the rest. Not Sandy. She would overwhelm you with her knowledge." Senator O'Connor was also skilled at bringing people into agreement. One associate from her senate days called her a "wizard" at hammering out compromises between parties.

Though she worked very long hours while she was

in the senate, Mrs. O'Connor tried never to neglect her family. Once, the legislature was meeting in the evening. Senator O'Connor left early, explaining, "My boys are going to camp and I am going home to be sure that they have packed everything." Her family was as usual a source of strength to Mrs. O'Connor. Her husband always helped her and encouraged her efforts.

Sandra O'Connor also managed to find time to pursue her outside interests. Among other things, she was on the board of Arizona's Heard Museum, where she did outstanding work detailing the accomplishments of the Indian tribes who played a major role in the history of Arizona. One of the board members recalls her as being dedicated and unpretentious. Once, they had a dinner at the luxurious University Club. Sandra O'Connor arrived at the club and sat at the dinner table, but she ignored the menu. The only request she made to the waiter was for a clean plate and a glass of water. After the startled waiter honored her unusual order, she calmly dug into her purse and extracted a can of water-packed tuna fish! That was her lunch, she explained, because she was on a diet.

Sandra O'Connor also declined to use her influence in Arizona society for her own benefit. Once, when the Heard Museum was having a sale of handicrafts, she went to the sale and found a huge line of people waiting to purchase their favorite objects. Instead of using her influence as a member of the board of directors to go to the head of the line, Sandra O'Connor waited patiently for her turn. Typically, she had come prepared for any situation; she had brought a camp stool to sit down on!

Though she didn't put on a show, Senator O'Connor was rapidly rising in the eyes of her fellow Republicans. In 1972, she was appointed an alternate delegate to the party's national convention, where she supported the renomination of Richard M. Nixon for president of the United States.

In 1973 Sandra Day O'Connor made her first "first" in U.S. history. She finally felt accomplished enough to run for the post of senate majority leader. Her colleagues agreed with her, and she became the first woman in the country to become the majority leader of a state legislature. Of her election, Mary Ellen Simonson, a legislative aide at the time, later said to a reporter, "She's finished at the top in a lot of things. She has a reputation for excellence. As a result she's been one of the state's leading role models for women."

However much of an honor it is to have the title "majority leader," the real test comes in being able to do the job on a day-to-day basis. A state senate is a place where decisions are made concerning huge amounts of money. There are many special-interest groups who constantly try to influence the thinking of the senators. Also, the legislators themselves are not the kind of people who are easily persuaded on any matter. In a state senate, one will frequently find men and women with strong convictions.

It didn't take Sandra O'Connor very long to realize that her new job required a degree of toughness that she wasn't accustomed to exercising. She later said about her time in the senate, "It was a totally different experience [from the attorney general's office] and it was more difficult and more controversial. It was the kind of job where you would have many confrontations with people. People cared very deeply about issues, and might disagree with you and want to express their disagreements in strong ways."

ᴄ Being majority leader tested Sandra O'Connor's negotiating abilities as nothing else had. She had to know when to call a vote and when to hold back. As in many organizations where many people hold strong opinions, Senator O'Connor had her share of disagreements. Once a male member of the senate became angry with her. He said, "If you were a man, I'd punch you in the nose." Maybe he expected her to break into tears over this undignified remark, but she didn't. Instead, she told him, "If you were a man, you could."

Sandra O'Connor was supported during her most trying days in the senate by the knowledge that she was doing the best possible job for the people of Arizona. Years later, after she was nominated for a seat on the Supreme Court, she telephoned Burton Barr, who was the current house majority leader in her home state. Mr. Barr told Sandra O'Connor to show people in Washington conducting the nomination hearings her record in the Arizona state senate. He felt that her accomplishments there would easily convince the legislators in Washington that she was perfect for the Supreme Court position. He told her during that phone conversation, "When you get down there [in Washington], tell them that we have the best set of state laws in the country and that you helped draw them up."

Chapter/Four

"...A marvelous experience with a new branch of government."

Instead of running for re-election when her second term was over in the legislature, Sandra Day O'Connor decided that she would be happier in the judicial branch of the government. Through she had handled the give and take of the senate with ease, she had also felt the constant tension that comes from dealing with people who hold strong, opposing opinions. Also, she had been a lawyer but never a judge, and she thought she would enjoy the experience of a courtroom from the other side of the bench.

Her move from one branch of the government to another would not necessarily be easy for her. The judgeship that she eyed was not an appointed position. She would have to campaign and be elected to it. Furthermore, despite her popularity with the people she represented in the senate, other people in Arizona were not that familiar with her. No one could predict that she would be successful in running for a judgeship.

However, Sandra Day O'Connor never failed to face a challenge. Disregarding advice to play it safe and continue her rise up the political ladder, in 1974 Senator O'Connor ran for the position of trial judge. The election proved to be a particularly hard-fought contest, but she won. Sandra Day O'Connor became a judge of the Maricopa County Superior Court. She would remain there for five years.

Serving as a trial judge is very different from working in the legislature. Instead of debating the wording or philosophy of a law, a judge faces real individuals and specific human situations. A judge must evaluate people's actions and the consequences of those actions in light of the law. In some senses, it is easier to write a law for general application than to throw its weight towards an individual standing right in front of you.

The judge has to view the matter before the court as fairly as possible, taking into consideration the law that was broken and what effect it has on society. He or she also has to study the individuals involved and any circumstances that would lessen or add to the punishment that might be imposed. Of course, the prosecuting attorney, the defense lawyer, and the jury all share in the judicial process, contributing information and helping to evaluate the guilt or innocence of the defendant. However, in the end, only the presiding judge may make a decision on how society should deal with that particular individual and his or her crime. A judge may send someone to jail for the maximum amount of time that the law allows for a specific crime, or can impose a lighter sentence. A trial judge may also deal with civil matters, such as medical malpractice suits, contract disputes, and so forth. But whether the matter is civil or criminal, each day a trial judge makes decisions in court that will change the lives of people.

Judge O'Connor quickly developed a reputation for expecting only performances of the highest quality from both defending and prosecuting attorneys in her courtroom. At least twice she recommended that individuals on trial before her get someone else to represent them; she felt that their present lawyers were not adequately prepared for the trial. As always, Sandra Day O'Connor demanded the best from herself, and she expected the same from others.

It was common knowledge that Judge O'Connor was fair and honest. She took care to see that all of the proceedings in her courtroom were conducted in public, not in the privacy of her chambers. Attorneys quickly found out that Sandra O'Connor wasn't the type of judge with whom lawyers could make "backroom" deals. Everything she did had to be aboveboard, and according to the letter of the law.

This quality of honesty was noted by the press years later when Sandra O'Connor joined the Supreme Court. She submitted a financial statement, listing her property and savings, as did all the other justices. However, hers was so detailed that she even listed a $350 quilt she received as a present—along with the names of the thirty-one people who chipped in to purchase it for her!

Judge O'Connor was also honest enough to admit her own shortcomings. Once, she reversed her decision on a first-degree murder case after the defense lawyer pointed out a mistake she had made on the case. Both the defending and prosecuting attorneys were much impressed with Sandra O'Connor's humility.

Perhaps the most difficult case over which Judge O'Connor had to preside involved a woman who had cashed over three thousand dollars worth of bad checks. There were few circumstances which would lessen the guilt of the woman. The defendant came from a very good family; she had a master's degree; and she was known as a top real estate agent.

The punishment that should be given was a difficult problem, however. The woman had two young children, and she was unmarried. The older child was sixteen months old, and the younger one was only three weeks old. If Judge O'Connor sent the woman to jail, she would be depriving two very young children of their mother. Since no father was legally involved with the children, there was also the possibility that there might be no one willing to care for the infants while their mother was in jail. If so, the children would become wards of the state. In imposing a punishment on the mother for her crimes, Judge O'Connor might end up punishing the two children as well.

Before announcing her decision, she told the woman, "It is the most difficult case that I have had to resolve . . . . You have intelligence, beauty, and two small children. You come from a fine and respected family . . . . Someone with all of your advantages should have known better." Referring to the mother's plea to consider her children, Judge O'Connor added, "I believe that the words you have spoken are sincere. As a mother I know that they are." She then sentenced the woman to five to ten years in prison.

As Judge O'Connor left the court for her chambers, she could hear the woman she had just sentenced screaming over and over, "What about my babies? What about my babies?"

To some, solemn-faced Judge O'Connor appeared heartless in this case. However, a man who worked for the court at that time later reported Sandra O'Connor's true feelings. He entered her chambers shortly after the incident happened, and was shocked to see Judge O'Connor sitting at her desk crying. She had done what she believed she had to do in order to uphold the law. The employee said she was "bawling like a baby" from the strain.

However, there were often times when Judge O'Connor did consider the circumstances which surrounded a crime. She once gave a woman who was convicted of murder the shortest possible sentence. The woman had admitted murdering her husband, but she claimed that she did it in self-defense. The husband had often severely beaten her. Though the wife had broken the law, Judge O'Connor felt she deserved a lenient sentence. The judge was able to see beyond the law, and feel the plight of the individual who had committed the crime.

Sandra O'Connor has no regrets about her judgments in court or politics. She told one interviewer, "I've had to make many tough decisions as a trial court judge and as a legislator. I did my very best to consider all aspects of a question, but once I had made my decision known, I never consciously looked back."

As always, Sandra O'Connor continued to have

interests apart from the law while serving on the Maricopa County Court. Though she put in long hours both on and off the bench, she found time for a multitude of outside activities. She served on the board of Blue Cross-Blue Shield of Arizona (a medical insurance company) and was a trustee of her alma mater, Stanford University. She also enjoyed an active social life. Joel Smith, who was vice-president of Stanford University during those years, recalls that Mrs. O'Connor was "the best dancer I've ever danced with." Although she had a housekeeper, Sandra O'Connor kept up her interest in cooking. (She even entered a cooking contest during this time.) And, as always, she spent most of her time off with her family. She loved to swim and play tennis with her children.

A friend named Carolyn Warner recalls times the Warners and the O'Connors would get together. On Easter Sundays, the two families would often go to the Easter party at the Arizona Biltmore Hotel where, Sandra O'Connor had discovered, both parents and children could have a good time at the Biltmore's "Bunny Brunch." The hotel provided clowns and endless entertainment for the children. According to Mrs. Warner, "It was a great escape for parents from the usual [Easter] routine of baby chickens, rabbits, spoiled eggs, etc." She adds that the "Bunny Brunch" was an example of her friend Sandra O'Connor's talent for creative solutions which carries over from "the mundane world of raising children to the sublime world of the Supreme Court." She also says that she knows of no one better able to make the transition between the two lifestyles.

Judge O'Connor found her five years as a trial judge very satisfying. It gave her insights into how the judicial system works on a day-to-day basis, which would be most valuable when she was eventually appointed to the highest court in the country. While reflecting on her experiences in the courtroom, she would later say that those years were "a marvelous experience and with a new branch of government. I went from the executive branch in the attorney general's office to the legislative branch and finally to the judicial branch. It was a most interesting experience to be a trial court judge and see the multitude of cases that came before it."

By 1979, Judge O'Connor was so successful as a trial judge that some of her fellow Republicans urged her to be their candidate when they challenged Governor Bruce Babbit, a Democrat, in the next election. However, this never came to be; Governor Babbitt appointed Judge O'Connor to a position on the Arizona Court of Appeals. A few people suggested, only half jokingly, that Judge O'Connor's appointment was an effort to remove a possible political rival. Governor Babbitt responded by saying, "I had to find the finest talent available . . . . Her intellectual ability and her judgment are astonishing." Whatever the reason, Sandra O'Connor accepted the appointment.

Joining the Court of Appeals was, in a way, a promotion for Judge O'Connor. The Court of Appeals reviews cases that were previously tried in a lower court. A case is brought before an appeals court when someone believes there is a valid objection to a decision made by another judge or a jury. The defendant in a criminal case, for example, may appeal because he or she feels the jury was prejudiced or the judge acted unfairly. Someone who loses a civil lawsuit and is ordered to pay a large sum of money might appeal to have the amount of money reduced or the judgment thrown out altogether. In appellate cases, there is no jury. The judge alone reviews the records of the previous trial or trials and decides if the appeal has merit.

While she was on the Court of Appeals, Sandra Day O'Connor wrote twenty-nine opinions, or decisions. When an appeals court judge hands down a decision on a case, he or she must base the decision on the merits of the case. However, this must be done while looking at precedent—how similar cases were decided in the past by other judges. While Sandra O'Connor was an appellate judge, she didn't break any new ground; she interpreted the law strictly in accordance with decisions that were made in similar cases before other judges.

Throughout her career, Judge O'Connor has worked against courts becoming bogged down by minor points of law. If someone has broken a law, that person should be punished. In her thinking, the courts will lose their effectiveness if they become clogged and overcrowded by people appealing decisions because of small technical errors. She is not against people appealing their cases; she knows that the right of appeal is a built-in safety net, a system designed to protect the innocent from punishment and to correct unfair civil judgments. However, she does frown on people who attempt to use the appeals system to avoid justice.

Her experience in the legislative branch of govern-

ment was of great help to her while she was on the
Court of Appeals. Frequently, cases are appealed because a law has been badly worded by a legislature.
Such a statute might be interpreted in more than one
way. Laws like these inevitably lead to many appeals.
Whichever way a judge might rule, someone can say
that he or she misread the law, and take the case to an
appellate court. Badly written laws can quickly clog a
court system.

Because she had experience both as a legislator
and a judge, Sandra O'Connor was able to work on
both sides of the problem. While she was on the Court
of Appeals, Judge O'Connor frequently advised the
legislature about the effects that the wording of some
of their laws was having in the courts. Because she
understood the law-writing procedure, she was able to
guide the legislature on amendments that should be
made to several unclear laws. For instance, during her
term in appellate court she helped lawmakers revise statutes concerning unemployment insurance and
worker's compensation.

Most of the cases that came before Judge O'Connor's court were not monumental or precedent setting.
Most involved worker's compensation, divorce, bank-
ruptcies, tenant-landlord disputes, and appeals to over-
turn criminal convictions. Reporters who interviewed
Sandra O'Connor's colleagues on the Arizona Court
of Appeals found that her fine mind and strong charac-
ter were much appreciated during her service there.

Chapter/Five

"I did not know whether... I should accept it if I was offered the chance."

In June of 1981, Judge Sandra Day O'Connor was in the midst of her fifth term on the Arizona Court of Appeals. She didn't know that thousands of miles away, in Washington, D.C., events were set in motion that would eventually change the course of her life.

June was a busy month for staff members at the Reagan White House, though few outsiders were aware of additional activity. Associate Justice Potter Stewart, at age sixty-six and with twenty-three years experience on the Supreme Court, had told the president that the 1980-1981 term of the Supreme Court would be his last. However, he asked that his resignation not be announced at least until the middle of June.

Ronald Reagan respected his wishes, but he quietly asked members of his staff to draw up a list of possible replacements for Justice Stewart. Reagan told them to look for someone whose political and judicial philosophy were close to his own. However, he also said that he did not want any single issue to disqualify a candidate. If someone were highly suitable for the post but held an opposing view in one particular area, such as abortion or the Equal Rights Amendment, his or her name should still be included on this list.

President Reagan received a looseleaf binder labeled "eyes only" on June 23. Inside the binder was information on twenty-five people. Half of the candidates were women, a reflection of political reality in the 1980s. For the past twenty or thirty years, women have become more and more influential in our society. As the sexes advance towards equality in the workplace, there has been increasing pressure to have both women as well as men represented at the highest levels of government. Previously, Reagan had nominated few women to important positions in the government. The only woman in his administration who had a high-level post was Jeane Kirkpatrick, ambassador to the United Nations. This record of female appointments, as well as Reagan's opposition to the Equal Rights Amendment and abortion, had turned many women voters away from the Republican Party. It was clearly time for Mr. Reagan to fulfill his campaign pledge to nominate a woman to the first Supreme Court vacancy that he, as president, would have the opportunity to fill. One of the names on his list was an appeals court judge from Arizona—Sandra Day O'Connor.

However, the president could not nominate someone for such an important post just because she was a woman. He had to find someone who was able to do the job. He had previously qualified his pledge to appoint a woman by saying, "This is to not say that I would appoint a woman merely to do so. That would not be fair to women, nor to future generations of Americans whose lives are so deeply affected by decisions of the Court. Rather, I pledge to appoint a woman who meets the very high standards I demand of all Court appointees."

By the end of June the list of twenty-five candidates had been pared down to Judge O'Connor and three other women. Once the list of potential appointees was limited to four, it wasn't difficult for Reagan's staff to separate Sandra Day O'Connor from the rest. As one staff member who was instrumental in the final choice later told a reporter, "She really made it easy. She was the right age, had the right philosophy, the right combination of experience, the right political affiliation, the right backing."

Though Reagan didn't know her, many people whom he respected supported her as the nominee. His attorney general, William French Smith, enthusiastically defended her nomination. Both Smith and Sandra O'Connor had gone to Stanford Law School. The dean of Stanford Law, Charles Myers, also sang her praises. Perhaps more importantly, she was the choice of another Stanford graduate, William Rehnquist, the most recently appointed associate justice of the Supreme Court. Finally, the influential senator from Arizona, Barry Goldwater, pointed her out to the Reagan staff as the most qualified person on the list.

Sandra Day O'Connor was also politically acceptable to the Reagan administration. Though Court justices are supposed to be politically neutral, realistically, individual justices are influenced by their political philosophies. Some justices have a tendency to emphasize one aspect of the law, while other justices might emphasize another aspect.

Both Ronald Reagan and Sandra Day O'Connor were politically conservative. In general, a conservative is likely to stress the rights of local and state governments to make their own laws and regulations. A conservative also usually favors limiting the role of the federal government. In an article published in the *William and Mary Law Review*, Judge O'Connor clearly noted that federal courts are not necessarily better than state tribunals. "When the state court judge puts on his or her federal court robe," said Judge O'Connor, "he or she does not become immediately better equipped intellectually to do the job."

The president and Sandra Day O'Connor also had similar philosophies about how the court system should work. They believed that the important issues in court cases are often clouded because of overemphasis on trivial matters. President Reagan, like Justice O'Connor, felt that the courts had lost some of their effectiveness. They both cited cases where defendants have been freed because of a minor mistake by the police in their investigation and arrest procedures. In addition, they both believed that there have been instances in the past when defendants have abused their constitutional rights.

However promising Judge O'Connor looked to Ronald Reagan, he had to thoroughly investigate her background. Before her nomination was announced, he wanted to make sure that his appointee was a proper choice. He knew that political leaders, interest groups, and the press would surely conduct their own investigations into Sandra Day O'Connor's past. It would be embarrassing if his nominee proved unworthy of the office.

The first steps in the investigation were done very cautiously. The Justice Department sent a lawyer to Phoenix to gather background information on Sandra O'Connor. At the same time, the attorney general, William French Smith, spoke with Judge O'Connor a few times on the phone. She learned that she was being seriously considered by the president for such a high honor. "I was flabbergasted," she said.

A few days later, William French Smith sent two Justice Department lawyers to Phoenix to spend the day with Judge O'Connor and her family in the O'Connor home in Paradise Valley outside of Phoenix. During the day they questioned her in great detail about her personal life and her political philosophy. For this special occasion, Judge O'Connor served them a luncheon which she had prepared herself. She discussed her life with them over iced tea. The lawyers returned to Washington with a very favorable impression of the potential nominee.

While Reagan and his staff were trying to decide if she was appropriate for the job, Judge O'Connor was wondering if she should accept the appointment if it were offered to her. Though it would be a great honor to sit on the highest court of the land, it would also be a tremendous disruption to her life. Because the Supreme Court meets in Washington, D.C., she would have to move away from her Paradise Valley home. Her husband John, a partner in a Phoenix law firm, would have to leave his job in order to be with her. All the O'Connors would have to brace themselves for the media attention given to American public figures and their families.

There was also the job itself. By this time, both she and her family had already grown accustomed to her habit of working exceedingly long and hard hours to take care of whatever responsibilities her job held. On the Supreme Court, the responsibilities—and the work-load—would be much greater. Consequently, her commitment to work would have to be even greater than that she had displayed during her terms in the legislature and the Arizona judicial system.

Judge O'Connor had to consider more than the effect on her personal life. She also had to weigh her ability to do the job. Throughout her life, she had served the people of Arizona with dedication. She had always been a firm believer in and defender of the American system of government. Public service was not something that she did for personal gain or glory. She believed that American citizens must get involved in their government if it was going to work. Now she was being asked to serve, not only the people of Arizona, but the whole American population. Her decisions would affect the lives of millions of Americans. If she accepted the post of Supreme Court justice, she would be accepting a very great responsibility.

When she was asked later if it was difficult to decide whether or not to accept the nomination, she explained, "I had to view it with a lot of concern: about what it would mean for me and my family, to my life, and also whether I could do the job. It takes an enormous amount of ability and understanding to discharge this job well." Admitting her doubts, Judge O'Connor continued, "I did not know whether I thought it was appropriate that I should accept it if I was offered the chance."

By the end of June, President Reagan's list of possible nominees had only one name on it—Sandra Day O'Connor. She flew to Washington where she met with William French Smith at a breakfast. Smith was impressed with her, and he sent a favorable report to the White House.

The following day, she met with Edwin Meese, James Baker, Michael Deaver, and Fred Fielding, some of the President's top aides. The meeting was held in the L'Enfant Plaza Hotel in order to keep Sandra O'Connor's presence in Washington a secret from the press. They didn't want her to be spotted going in and out of the White House. The president hadn't made his final decision yet, and he wanted to be free from questions from the press until he did.

Sandra O'Connor's meeting with the White House aides was more difficult than the meeting with the attorney general on the previous day. The president's aides questioned her very closely. They already knew that she was qualified and had an excellent background for the job; that was not what they wanted to know. They wanted to see how well Judge O'Connor stood up under pressure. Any nominee to an important government position is subject to sharp questioning from both Congress and the press. Every aspect of the nominee's personal and professional life is challenged. Candidates—even worthy candidates—have been known to collapse in the face of such intense attention. The Reagan administration wanted to test Judge O'Connor in advance to be sure that she could withstand the trials of the nomination process. As one of the participants in the session said, "We were testing her psychological and intellectual stamina."

The interview lasted ninety minutes. The aides were impressed with Sandra Day O'Connor, but one more hurdle remained. On the following day, Judge O'Connor would have her final interview. It would be in the White House, and it would be with the president.

At ten o'clock, aides slipped Judge O'Connor past the White House press corps without anyone noticing. No one suspected that a historic meeting was taking place. Up to this point the president hadn't interviewed anyone for the position. He had taken an active role in limiting the original list to twenty-five potential nominees, but for interviewing he had relied exclusively on the work of his staff and of the Justice Department. Mr. Reagan himself had never actually met the people that his staff was investigating. From their reports, Mr. Reagan knew that Judge O'Connor looked very good "on paper." Nevertheless he had to meet her himself.

When they met, the president and Sandra O'Connor instantly felt at ease with one another. Judge O'Connor mentioned that she and the president had met ten years before, while he was governor of California and she was in the Arizona state senate. At that time, both states were considering bills to limit spending. Mr. Reagan smilingly told Sandra O'Connor, "Yours passed, but mine didn't."

The two found that they had many things in common. They both shared happy experiences from childhoods spent on Western ranches. They also shared similar political viewpoints. The meeting lasted forty-five minutes. One of the members of the Reagan's staff who was at the meeting called her a "real charmer." Reagan knew right away that he had found the perfect person for the job.

The day after the meeting, word was circulated to a few reporters that Sandra Day O'Connor was on the "short list" of candidates for the position on the Supreme Court. Presidents often "leak" information like this to the press so that they can sample public opinion on potential nominees. If there is an unfavorable reaction, the candidate's name can be withdrawn before he or she has actually been named. This saves the president the embarrassment of naming an unpopular person. As soon as Judge O'Connor's name was reported in the press, people began to send telegrams to the White House, commenting on her selection. The first batch of telegrams ran ten to one against Judge O'Connor. Several White House employees felt that she would never win the nomination.

Only a week later Sandra Day O'Connor was working in her office in Phoenix when the phone rang. The president himself was calling! He wanted to know if she would accept the nomination to the Court.

Sandra O'Connor said yes.

Chapter/Six

"Here Lies a Good Judge"

On July 7, 1981, the president announced that Sandra Day O'Connor was his nominee for the vacancy on the Supreme Court. In the announcement, Reagan said, "I pledged to appoint a woman who meets the very high standards I demand from all of my Court appointees. I have identified such a person." He described her as being "a woman for all seasons." Judge O'Connor responded by promising the American public that "... If confirmed, I will do my best to serve the court ... in a manner that will bring credit to the president ... and to all the people of this great nation."

When asked how she would affect the Court as the first woman to serve there, Judge O'Connor said, "I can only say I will approach [the work of the Court] with care and effort and do the best job that I can do." She also told reporters that she was "greatly honored" by the fact that she had been considered for the appointment. Several reporters noted that Judge O'Connor seemed nervous during her statement, though she handled herself with great dignity.

Reagan made the announcement with Sandra, John, and the O'Connor children present. Harry and Ada Mae Day, who could not speak to their daughter during her triumph because the Lazy B phone was out of order, watched her proudly on television. (The television was on almost constantly during the next few days at the ranch. Ada Mae Day told a reporter, "We just like to watch for news about her.") As the O'Connors left, a group of reporters and photographers descended upon them. Many wanted to snap pictures of the family. Scott, one of the O'Connor sons, suggested that the family skip saying "cheese" for the more appropriate "supreeeeeme." The reporters loved it.

Because she was the first woman ever considered for the Court, Sandra O'Connor's nomination was of great significance. People all across the country hailed her selection as a landmark in American history. Women's groups were particularly pleased. Eleanor Smeal, president of the National Organization of Women (NOW), called Judge O'Connor's nomination "a major victory for women's rights." Iris Mitgang, head of the National Women's Political Caucus, said the nomination was "a major step towards equal justice in our land." Many prominent politicians, such as Howard Baker, the senate majority leader, and Senator Strom Thurmond of South Carolina approved of the president's choice. Democratic Senator Edward Kennedy of Massachusetts stated, "Every American can take pride in the president's commitment to select such a woman for this critical office."

However, not everyone was happy with Sandra Day O'Connor's nomination. The first group to react negatively to President Reagan's announcement was the right-to-life movement. This group is strongly opposed to abortion, supporting what they believe is an unborn child's right to life. It was members of this group who had sent telegrams to the White House opposing Judge O'Connor after her name had been leaked to the press. For the most part, right-to-life groups had supported President Reagan in the 1980 election, partly because they believed he would take any steps in his power as president to limit or end abortions. Consequently, they expected any Reagan nominee to the Supreme Court to be firmly opposed to abortion. They were quite disappointed when Sandra Day O'Connor was named because they felt her record did not show a clear anti-abortion position. They accused her of voting against "pro-life" legislation and of speaking at a pro-abortion conference.

Many of the right-to-life groups' accusations were difficult to prove because of the nature of the legislative process. In one example, they accused Judge O'Connor of voting against an anti-abortion amendment to a sports bill. She did vote against the amendment, but not because she was pro-abortion. The reason was simply that the amendment was attached to a sports bill! According to the Constitution of Arizona, an amendment to a bill has to have something to do with the bill that is being amended; therefore, any amendment to a sports bill would have to be related to sports. Justice O'Connor explained that when she voted against the amendment, she was merely upholding the constitution she had sworn to follow.

Still another charge concerned a family-planning bill that Sandra O'Connor had sponsored while in the Arizona state senate. The bill provided that "all medically acceptable family-planning methods and information" were to be available to anyone who wanted them. The right-to-life groups believed that "all medically acceptable" methods included abortion. Judge O'Connor answered that criticism by stating that there was no specific mention of abortion in the bill she had sponsored, and abortion had not been her intention when she voted in its favor.

As anti-abortion forces became more vocal, other people were angered by the criticism they directed against Judge O'Connor. Finally Barry Goldwater, a conservative Republican senator from Arizona, spoke out against Sandra O'Connor's critics. He told them to "back off," saying angrily, "Instead of jumping to conclusions about her views on the basis of years-old positions that were taken in a different context [setting], why can't these people wait until the nomination hearings?" Mr. Goldwater, who said he has known Sandra O'Connor "for so many years I can't count them" believes that he has never known, "in my life, anyone more dedicated to the idea of service." He has often remarked that Sandra O'Connor is "one of the most complete women I've ever known in my life."

Many other people defended Judge O'Connor's nomination, pointing out that a Supreme Court justice has to deal with a wide range of issues. By focusing only on abortion, they said, Sandra Day O'Connor's critics were unable to see the breadth of her experience and her ability in other areas.

Yet opposition continued to build against Sandra O'Connor's nomination. Before the start of her nomination hearings, a coalition of twenty-one conservative and anti-abortion groups publicly stated that Judge O'Connor's voting record was unacceptable to them.

As controversy swirled around her, Sandra O'Connor remained in Arizona. Friends described her office in the Arizona Court of Appeals as being (most uncharacteristically) in utter chaos. Everywhere one looked there were bouquets of flowers that admirers had sent. Someone, presumably thinking of President Reagan's fondness for jelly beans, had mailed the nominee to the Court a jar of the candies. Her desk was also covered with papers and files. The room was crowded with people who were helping her review all of her cases in preparation for the hearings. Judge O'Connor had to be ready to answer questions about every single legal decision she had ever made—not an easy task. Her husband, her friends, and law clerks were all there assisting her in the monumental task of review. As she said at the time, "It's a nightmare. Fifty years is a long time. It's hard to remember everything that you did."

Meanwhile, the press was doing its own research. They peppered her colleagues and friends with questions about her personality, habits, and beliefs. Slowly they pieced together a portrait of a woman who was hard working, dedicated, and demanding. One friend, Paul Eckstein, told a reporter that, "She's pretty independent. Those people who are supporting her may be surprised by her, and those people who are opposing her may come to like her." William Jacquin, who had served in the Arizona senate with Sandra O'Connor, told one journalist that the judge was a "super floor leader . . . devoted to the law by the nature of her own professionalism and . . . extraordinarily thorough in drafting legislation."

Though the congressional hearings on her appointment weren't scheduled to start until the beginning of September, Judge O'Connor traveled to Washington on August 14 to meet with Justice Department personnel. The conferences were designed to prepare her for possible questions. As Judge O'Connor arrived for the meeting, she was greeted by an anti-abortion demonstration outside.

She spent the rest of the week meeting with important officials in Washington. She made courtesy calls on such people as senators Barry Goldwater and Thomas "Tip" O'Neill, and members of the Senate Judiciary Committee. On August 16, an encouraging Associated Press/NBC poll was released. According to the poll, 65 percent of the American people approved of her appointment, and only 6 percent disapproved. The rest had no opinion. The survey showed that men as well as women supported her nomination. Judge O'Connor returned to Arizona after meeting the senators, commenting that their friendliness was "a very encouraging feeling." She added, "It will give me hope."

One week before her confirmation hearings were scheduled to begin, Judge O'Connor submitted a written statement outlining her financial holdings and beliefs to the Senate Judiciary Committee. The financial statement revealed that the newest candidate for the Supreme Court and her husband were millionaires, owning, among other things, a house in Paradise Valley, an interest in Mr. O'Connor's law firm, and a share of the family ranch, the Lazy B. If confirmed, Judge O'Connor would be one of the wealthier members of the Court. Her statement of beliefs also reaffirmed Sandra O'Connor's view that judges should simply interpret the law as it is written, and not try to change society by creating new laws. As she said in her report, "Judges are not only not authorized to engage in executive or legislative functions, but they are also ill-equipped to do so."

On September 9, the hearings began. Sandra O'Connor began by introducing her husband John and three sons to the eighteen male senators on the committee. She affirmed that John O'Connor had been "enthusiastically supportive of this whole nomination and this endeavor." She told the panel that marriage was "the hope of the world and the strength of the country." Judge O'Connor said again that the function of the judiciary was to "interpret and apply the law, not make it." She also said, "As the first woman to be nominated as a Supreme Court justice, I am particularly honored, but I happily share the honor with millions of American women of yesterday and today whose abilities and conduct have given me this opportunity of service."

She was very careful when she was asked to explain her position on various issues, refusing to comment in detail on any matter she felt might come before the Court. In her opening statement, Sandra O'Connor said: "I do not believe that, as a nominee, I can tell you how I might vote on a particular issue which may come before the Court, or endorse or criticize specific Supreme Court decisions presenting issues which may well come before the Court again. To do so would mean I have prejudged the matter or have morally committed myself to a certain position."

When pressed about her opinion on the legality of abortion, Judge O'Connor said, "My own view is that I am opposed to abortion either as birth control or otherwise." However, she added that, "I'm over the hill. I'm not going to be pregnant anymore, so it's perhaps easy for me" to hold that position. She also said that she realized she had an "obligation to recognize that others have different views."

Conservative Senator Jeremiah Denton questioned Mrs. O'Connor about abortion for thirty minutes, trying to get her to make a stronger statement on the controversial issue. When the committee chair, Strom Thurmond of South Carolina, asked Mr. Denton if he wanted extra time to question Judge O'Connor, Denton replied, "I don't know if another month would do."

Sandra O'Connor also commented on crime during the hearings, noting that, "The public is very, very distressed about crime," and implying that she might favor tighter bail laws, especially for those who have already been convicted of previous offenses. When asked about sex discrimination, Judge O'Connor mentioned that she had not been able to find a job after graduating from Stanford Law School. She stated that sex discrimination has "always been a matter of concern to me," and told the senators that while in Arizona she had actively tried to reform laws that discriminated against women.

During the hearings, Judge O'Connor leaned forward in her chair, listening intently and answering the senators' questions in a serious tone of voice. There was one light moment, however, when she was asked how she would like to be remembered. She jokingly replied, "Ah, the tombstone question!" Then she became serious and added, "I hope that it says, 'Here Lies A Good Judge.'"

After Judge O'Connor had finished her testimony, a number of other witnesses spoke to the committee. A representative of the American Bar Association, a lawyers' group, told the senators that the organization felt Judge O'Connor was qualified for the post on the Supreme Court, even though she was not as experienced as some other candidates. Many anti-abortion advocates also spoke at the hearings, though the senators did not always appear to give such witnesses their full attention. In fact, many of the committee members left the hearing room while the right-to-life representatives were talking. By midafternoon of the third day of testimony, only the committee chair, Senator Thurmond, remained in the chamber.

The press was generally favorable to Judge O'Connor's performance in her confirmation hearings, though some criticized her refusal to give specific opinions on the most controversial issues of the day. Most, however, agreed with Julia Malone, who wrote in the *Christian Science Monitor* that: "Mrs. O'Connor struck an even balance of professionalism and femininity."

On September 22, her appointment was discussed in the Senate. The legislators had set aside four hours to debate her qualifications. However, Sandra O'Connor was so popular that there was almost no discussion needed. Many senators were absent, and those who were there took turns praising President Reagan's nominee. Senator Strom Thurmond, for example, said that "Judge O'Connor is extraordinarily well-qualified to serve on the Supreme Court." Barry Goldwater noted that Sandra O'Connor could quote previous Supreme Court decisions "as easily as most people would recite their birthdates."

After the four hours were up, the senators filed in for the vote. The final tally was 99 to 0 in favor of Sandra Day O'Connor. (There are a hundred senators, but one was absent on the day of the vote.) Minutes after the vote, she appeared on the Capitol steps with Vice-President George Bush, Attorney General Smith, and some of the senators. She told a group of supporters, "My hope is that ten years from now, after I've been across the street at work [in the Supreme Court building] for a while, they'll all be glad they gave me that wonderful vote."

Chapter/Seven

"... To administer justice without respect to persons and with equal rights to the poor and the rich."

After she was confirmed, Sandra returned with John O'Connor to Phoenix to prepare for the move to Washington. Although it has been usual for wives to follow husbands when the husband's career requires a move to a new state, many husbands would hesitate at the idea of following their wives in the reverse situation. Not John O'Connor. He immediately resigned from his law firm and began to look for a position in Washington. He quickly found a place with the law firm of Miller and Chevalier. When asked if it was difficult to leave Phoenix on his wife's account, John O'Connor gave an emphatic denial. He and Sandra had been married for twenty-nine years, he said, and he wanted to continue to live with her. His only wish was that all the decisions facing him in life would be that easy! He also added, with characteristic humor, that he was now a member of a very exclusive club—the husbands of members of the Supreme Court.

Mr. O'Connor feels that his wife's rise in the world has enriched his own life as well. He told one magazine that he is "not only happy for Sandra because she is so competent and so deserving, but I am happy for myself and my family because all our lives have become more interesting. Sandra's accomplishments don't make me a lesser man; they make me a fuller man."

Mr. O'Connor's wholehearted support for his wife's new career was evident after the Senate hearings were over. Sandra O'Connor received many tributes during her last few days in Phoenix—parades, parties, and even a mock confirmation hearing. Through it all John O'Connor was at her side.

On September 25, 1981, Sandra Day O'Connor was sworn in as an associate justice of the Supreme Court. The brief ceremony took place in the stately Supreme Court building. The oath of office was administered by Chief Justice Warren Burger. She swore "to administer justice without respect to persons, and with equal rights to the poor and to the rich." John Jay O'Connor and the three O'Connor sons were there to witness Sandra's triumph, as was President Reagan and the retiring justice, Potter Stewart.

After she had been sworn in, the newest justice, wearing her black judicial robe from the Arizona Court of Appeals, posed in the inner yard of the building with President and Mrs. Reagan, Chief Justice Burger and Mrs. Burger, and the O'Connor family. Many Supreme Court employees waved to her from the surrounding windows, and she waved back. Then Justice O'Connor left the Supreme Court building with Chief Justice Burger. As they emerged into the

Washington sunlight and descended the broad marble steps in front of the building, reporters, television crews, and well-wishers were there to greet them. The chief justice said to the crowd, "You've never seen me with a better-looking justice, have you?" A reporter asked Justice O'Connor how she felt now that the ceremony was over, and she replied, "Just great!" (A slight breeze billowed the two justices' wide sleeves against each other. One magazine found it necessary to remark that Chief Justice Burger and Justice O'Connor were not holding hands!)

Justice O'Connor's first few weeks in Washington were quite hectic. She and her husband had to find an apartment—one large enough for the whole family to visit. Since she had no household help yet, she had to do all the cooking and cleaning herself. With typical consideration, she also answered some four thousand letters she had received from well-wishers and admirers. John O'Connor and a secretary helped her with this enormous task. Of course, she also had to begin her job at the Court. This was difficult in the beginning because the procedures of the Court, and even the physical layout of the building, were new to her.

Justice O'Connor also had to cope with pressures other new Supreme Court justices never face. As one magazine stated, Sandra Day O'Connor was the hundred-and-second member of the Court, but its first media phenomenon. Besides bearing the grave responsibilities of her high office, Justice O'Connor has had to bear the burden of being a celebrity. During the hearings, her picture appeared regularly in magazines, newspapers, and on television news shows all across

the country. In a very short time, she became nation-
ally famous.

As she became more and more familiar to Americans, Sandra O'Connor was unable to step outside of
her house without causing a stir. "Initially, when the
nomination first took place," says Justice O'Connor,
" . . . I would be recognized wherever I went. People
would come up and they would want to talk with me.
They would want autographs and they would want to
have some personal conversation or contact. This was
whether I was in the supermarket doing my shopping
or in the airport or wherever it might be."

This could be embarrassing and awkward at times.
"Any appearance that I made resulted in a great cluster
of people being around and it made it difficult to do
anything," remarks Sandra O'Connor. For example,
she was in line at the supermarket once, waiting for the
cashier to ring up her purchases. The man behind her,
recognizing the newest justice of the Supreme Court,
was carefully examining and announcing her purchases. He noticed everything, including a can of luncheon meat she had selected! Another time, Justice
O'Connor and her family were approached during a
Fourth of July outing by some patriotic vacationers.
They asked the justice to read the Declaration of Inde-
pendence aloud to them, to celebrate our country's
freedom. Justice O'Connor agreed, giving some lucky
Americans an experience they will always remember.

Fortunately, as the years have gone by, Americans
have become more used to the idea of a female justice
of the Supreme Court, and the media has focused its
attention elsewhere for the most part. "Now as I go

about my personal affairs," she says, "there is some recognition, but not as extensive as it first was, and I must say, it is much more pleasant to have some anonymity in life than it is to be faced with a high recognition level."

However, Sandra Day O'Connor is still a famous woman. Many young men and women throughout the country look up to her as someone who has worked hard throughout her life and earned the success she now enjoys. To some, Justice O'Connor is also proof that discrimination against women in America can be overcome. To others, Justice O'Connor is simply a distinguished figure in law, someone to turn to for advice and guidance in a similar career.

To this day, Sandra O'Connor receives a great many letters and telegrams. "There are many people who want to write me letters about things or want to meet with me or want some contact," she says. "I get many letters and inquiries from young people of school age. They are doing research papers or some other work and I really enjoy hearing from them. And it would be nice to be able to answer all their questions. But I frankly don't have the time. And that's a little bit of a frustration to me because I know as a student how much I would want to get a reply to my questions if I had taken the time to write. I am sure it is difficult for them to understand that, because I receive so many, I can't possibly respond to most of them." Adults also write to Justice O'Connor, inviting her to give lectures, attend fund-raising events, and even to preside over "moot courts." (A moot court is a kind of mock trial in which interesting cases are argued by law students.)

The presence of a woman on the Supreme Court of the United States required some adjustment on the part of the other eight justices, but for the most part the transition was remarkably smooth. Even before Sandra O'Connor was nominated, the members of the Court knew that it was likely a woman would soon join their ranks. Consequently, in November, 1980, they abandoned an old Supreme Court custom before it could create problems for a new, female member. Traditionally, the justices were addressed as "Mr. Justice White," "Mr. Justice Marshall," and so forth. The year before Sandra O'Connor was nominated, that was shortened to a plain "Justice White," and "Justice Marshall," so Sandra O'Connor became simply, "Justice O'Connor" after she was sworn in. Another point of etiquette that cropped up was the handshake the justices exchange at social functions. The male justices were in the habit of shaking their colleagues' hands and kissing the judges' wives at parties and other gatherings. They decided to shake both Sandra and John O'Connor's hands in those situations!

Her family gathered around Sandra Day O'Connor when news of her Supreme Court nomination was made public. From left, Jay, Brian, Sandra, John, and Scott O'Connor posed in Sandra's Appeals Court chambers.

After her Supreme Court nomination, Sandra Day O'Connor became, as a magazine put it, the Court's first media phenomenon. Photographers followed her everywhere, even to this meeting with friend and supporter Senator Barry Goldwater.

During her Senate confirmation hearings, Sandra O'Connor impressed many people with her logic, her record of achievements, and her grace under pressure, especially Senator Strom Thurmond and Attorney General William French Smith, with her here. The Senate confirmed her Supreme Court nomination 99 to 0.

Before the public ceremony, Sandra Day O'Connor was sworn in privately as the one-hundred-second justice of the Supreme Court. Chief Justice Warren Burger administered the oath of office, while John O'Connor held the Bibles on which the oath was sworn.

Newly-sworn-in Justice Sandra Day O'Connor and Chief Justice Burger walked down the Supreme Court building steps to speak to reporters after ceremonies in the courtyard of the building.

Sandra O'Connor's colleagues on the Bench: in the front row, from left, are Justice Thurgood Marshall, Justice William Brennan, Chief Justice Warren Burger, Justice Byron White, and Justice Harry A. Blackmun. Standing, from left, are Justice John Paul Stevens, Justice Lewis F. Powell, Jr., Justice William Rehnquist, and Justice O'Connor.

At work in her Supreme Court chambers, Justice O'Connor must here form her judgments on cases that affect many Americans' lives and livelihoods.

In 1984, Chief Justice Burger and Justice O'Connor were invited to London to participate in talks with British Prime Minister Margaret Thatcher. Both women are proof that today it is possible for women of accomplishment to achieve their dreams.

Chapter/Eight

"...A total commitment to the work."

Of course, the real importance of Justice O'Connor's arrival at the Court is not the handshakes, titles, or polite gesture, but the legal work she does there. Despite the fact that the actions of the judicial branch of our government have great influence over American life, few people understand exactly how the Supreme Court functions.

During the Court term, which runs from the first Monday in October until the following summer, the Court normally hears cases from Monday through Wednesday, for a period of two weeks. Then the justices spend two weeks on paperwork related to their cases before returning to court for more hearings.

While the Court is in session, Sandra Day O'Connor's workday begins hours before the official opening of the first case at ten o'clock in the morning. One of the first things on Justice O'Connor's schedule is the exercise class led by a teacher from the YWCA.

Dressed in leotards, Justice O'Connor and several women law clerks and female employees meet in the Supreme Court gym for a forty-five minute workout. It is a welcome change from the quiet, intellectual work that occupies most of her day.

After a quick shower and change of clothes, the justice is back in her office, preparing for the day's cases. To an outsider, it may seem as if there is not much work to do. The Supreme Court receives about five thousand applications a year but agrees to hear only about a hundred and fifty cases. Unless the case is extremely important, it is allotted only one hour of Court time—a half hour for the arguments in favor of the petition, and a half hour for the arguments against the petition. The one hundred fifty hours of Court time, however, are only the tip of the iceberg.

First of all, each judge reads all the documents dealing with the case. These include the records of the trials in lower courts. The Supreme Court is similar to an appeals court in that most of its cases have already been tried in a state or a federal court, and a verdict has already been given. The loser in the case, dissatisfied by the decision of the lower courts, appeals to the highest court to change the verdict. Since the Supreme Court is the final chance to change a court's decision, a case that is defeated there can go no higher. There is no jury; the nine justices vote, and their decision must be accepted. The Supreme Court also hears cases in which one state sues another or a state sues the federal government. Those cases, which are very rare, are extremely time-consuming. The record of one 1952 dispute between Arizona and California about Colorado River water rights was over 26,000 pages long! The Court also hears cases involving foreign diplomats or ambassadors.

Besides records of previous trials, the nine justices must read all the briefs connected with the case. A brief is a written explanation of all the laws and previous legal decisions that might be relevant to a case. They are submitted by both attorneys who will argue the case, as well as by any people with special interest in the outcome of a particular case. These extra briefs are called *amicus* briefs, a term derived from the Latin word for friend. After reviewing this material, the Supreme Court justices often have their law clerks prepare informational memos about each case. The clerks are young lawyers, often honor graduates of the best law schools, who assist the justices by doing legal research. A clerkship at the Court is a great honor because of the valuable experience a young lawyer gains there. Several former clerks have gone on to become Supreme Court justices themselves. Justices Byron White, William Rehnquist, and John Paul Stevens all began their careers as Supreme Court clerks. Though it is an honor, a Supreme Court clerkship is also a lot of work. The clerks often put in time on weekends, nights, and holidays to prepare the required reports. After studying all the written material, the justices may discuss each case with the law clerks before the arguments in court.

Justice O'Connor does most of the necessary paperwork in her chambers, or offices. Justice O'Connor's chambers occupy two spacious rooms on the ground floor of the building. The inner room, which is

Justice O'Connor's personal office, is lined with law texts. A beautiful black marble fireplace dominates one wall; in front of it is a small woven Indian rug. A comfortable black leather couch for visitors and several chairs are at one end of the room; on the other side is the judge's desk. Several vases filled with flowers brighten the room, as well as photographs of Justice O'Connor and her family. On the wall in the outer office, where Justice O'Connor's clerks and secretary work, is the framed front page of an Arizona paper announcing her nomination to the Court. Eight signed photos of the other justices line another wall. Justice O'Connor's office, like those of all the members of the Court, is equipped with a word processor. Until 1969, the Court relied solely on typewriters for its massive paperwork. Having to read carbon copies of every memo strained the justices' eyes, and drafts (proposed versions) of each decision had to be printed in the basement printing shop. Every single change meant reprinting the opinion. Now, each justice has an individual word processor connected to a central computer. Memos and other information can be sent to another justice with the touch of a button.

At five minutes before ten o'clock, a warning bell sounds in each justice's chamber signaling that a Court session is about to begin. The justices proceed to the robing room and put on their black robes. Dressed for court, they go to the conference room. This room, next door to the chief justice's chambers, is where the nine members of the Court meet to discuss cases. The justices also assemble there before Court sessions.

A brief ritual takes place in the conference room.

Each justice shakes hands with the other eight. This custom began nearly a hundred years ago. The chief justice at the time, Melville Fuller, said that the handshakes were a sign that all the justices had the same purpose in the courtroom, even if their opinions on a particular case differed.

At ten o'clock, led by Chief Justice Warren Burger, the justices enter the courtroom. The courtroom is a majestic room. The walls are marble, as are the tall columns that line the sides of the room. The high ceiling is carved with a rosette flower design. On the south wall are carved figures of Hammurabi, Confucius, Moses, and other early lawgivers. Napoleon, Mohammed, and later historical lawgivers top the north wall. Opposite the justices' bench are sculptures of the powers of Evil opposed by the powers of Good, as well as figures representing Justice, Wisdom, and Truth. The front wall of the court is covered with rich, red velvet draperies. In front of the draperies stands a high, mahogany bench with nine chairs behind it. The chairs are not uniform; each suits the preference of the justice who sits in it. The justices sit according to their seniority on the Court, with Chief Justice Warren Burger in the center and the next senior justices on either side of him. Justice O'Connor, who is the newest justice, sits on the far right as the spectator faces the bench. Her nearest neighbor is William Rehnquist, her former classmate from Stanford Law School.

In front of the bench are tables for lawyers and a tall podium at which each lawyer stands when he or she presents a case. There is a warning light on the podium which glows when a lawyer has used nearly all the allotted time. There are also desks for the clerk and marshall of the Court. The clerk is responsible for the Court calendar and supervises the printing of Supreme Court documents. The marshall is in charge of Court finances, ceremonies, and receptions, as well as the Supreme Court security forces. Both wear formal dress when the Court is in session.

The remainder of the room is for the use of spectators, who sit on wooden benches that resemble pews in a church. Only those who are properly dressed are admitted to the Court (though the rule that all lawyers must button their suit jackets is no longer enforced!) Uniformed ushers bring visitors to their seats and keep order. Spectators are expected to remain quiet and respectful during the Court proceedings. Ushers politely explain to visitors that arms and elbows may not be draped across the back of a bench, and no talking is allowed. In spite of these rules, the Supreme Court is a popular tourist attraction. Each day, hundreds of visitors line up outside the marble Court building for a chance to see one branch of the United States government in action. They are joined inside by reporters and people with special interest in the case being argued.

As the justices take their seats, the marshall announces, "Oyez, Oyez, Oyez. All persons having business before the honorable, the Supreme Court of the United States, are admonished to draw near and give their attention, for the Court is now sitting. God save the United States and this honorable Court." ("Oyez" is a French expression meaning "hear ye" and was used in old English courts.)

The spectators rise as the marshall speaks, and the Court is in session. Before the day's first case is heard, a new group of lawyers may be admitted to the Bar of the Supreme Court. This lets a lawyer practice before the Supreme Court. Many lawyers apply for admittance, whether or not they will ever plead a case in Washington. Some are admitted in person; they are given a ceremonial goose-quill pen as a souvenir. Others simply apply for and receive their admittance in the mail. Lawyers who argue a case before the Court are at the height of their careers. It is considered a great honor to practice before the Supreme Court. Once a lawyer has been "admitted to the Bar of the Court" he or she is called a "friend of the Court."

After that, opinions or decisions on previous cases may be announced. The Supreme Court's opinions are very important to all the other courts in the country. When interpreting a law or deciding a case, a judge in a lower court will often need to read the Supreme Court's opinion for guidance. So the opinion of the Supreme Court on a particular case will often be many pages long, explaining why the Court made the decision, and mentioning other cases and laws that influenced the Court's opinion.

Each Court decision names those justices who agree with the majority, and those who disagree. The senior justice of the majority assigns a member of the group to write the opinion for the group. The senior justice of the minority assigns the writing of the dissent, or disagreeing opinion. Justices may also write their own opinions if they feel the majority or minority opinions did not completely explain their own beliefs.

After the opinions have been summarized, it is time for current cases to be heard. The lawyers' speeches to the Court are called oral arguments. Though each attorney has a prepared speech, he or she may not have a chance to complete it exactly as planned. The nine justices listen attentively and interrupt whenever they please. This is not considered impolite in the procedures of the Court. In fact, it is a time-saving device. A justice can ask a question immediately when something needs to be explained, instead of waiting for a set speech to end. However, it is a little hard on the attorneys. They must really be able to think on their feet! In an instant, they must answer questions posed by the top legal minds of the day. Nevertheless, it does give the attorney a chance to address exactly those issues that conern the nine justices.

While the oral arguments proceed, the justices often send for law books, notes, or files that are necessary to the case. Messengers sit behind the justices and bring whatever they require. Some justices lean back in their chairs as they listen to the arguments; Sandra O'Connor sits upright or bends forward, intent on every word. Occasionally William Rehnquist will make a quiet comment to her.

After two cases are heard, the morning session is over and it is time for lunch. Those who imagine the justices lunching at an elegant Washington club are mistaken. Many eat a simple meal in the justices' dining room. (Justice O'Connor does not have extravagant eating habits. Even at the luncheon in her honor before she was sworn in, she turned down a glass of wine and requested diet soda. Supreme Court aides scurried to find some, and finally located a can in a vending machine.)

After lunch it is time for more paperwork. The justices may answer mail or write memos to the other justices, explaining their thoughts on a particular case. Since each judge's opinion may evolve during the time a particular case is considered, more than one memo to the other eight justices is often necessary.

At 12:55 p.m. the bell rings again, and the justices assemble for afternoon arguments. They hear two more cases, concluding at 3:00. Two days a week, the justices then attend a meeting in the conference room. The meetings allow the justices the opportunity to express their views on the various cases they are considering. To someone who hasn't studied law, it may seem as if there is nothing to discuss. The law often seems cut and dried, with a single, exact meaning. However, no matter how clearly it is worded, every law may be understood and applied in several different ways. Moreover, the Supreme Court is charged with safeguarding the United State Constitution. The Court may measure a law against the Constitution's principles and then declare it unconstitutional. Yet the Constitution is only a few pages long. It was written when our country consisted of only thirteen small, mostly agricultural states. Now the Court applies the Constitution's principles to situations the founders of our country never dreamed of, such as home taping of television shows, wiretapping, and so forth. Clearly there is room for individual interpretation.

At the conference, the chief justice typically begins the discussion. When he or she is finished, the senior associate justice speaks. Then, the other justices speak in order of seniority.

Traditionally, details of the discussions of each case are kept strictly secret. While the conference is in session, only the nine justices are allowed in the room. Even secretaries, messengers, and clerks are banned to ensure privacy. Following Supreme Court custom, the least senior justice is the conference's link to the outside world, answering the door or sending messages

The conferences last about two hours. After that, Justice O'Connor continues to read, study, and write about the cases for an hour or two more in her chambers. Then she goes home, but not without a stack of legal homework that must be completed that evening. Occasionally, Justice O'Connor and her husband will take time from their busy schedule for an evening out. They enjoy dancing and socializing with other Washingtonians. They have proved so popular that one national magazine stated definitely that they were on every Washington hostess's "A" list for a good party! At other times, the O'Connors themselves entertain. Visiting Arizonans often bring Sandra O'Connor fresh tortillas (corn pancakes). She uses the tortillas to make a specialty of the O'Connor kitchen: crabmeat enchiladas.

Clearly, the life of a Supreme Court justice is not an easy one. Though Sandra O'Connor has little time at home, she does not feel the same family-career tug that she would have earlier. "My present job is a total commitment to the work. Luckily, my children are now at an age when they wouldn't be at home in any event. And so I no longer have obligations to meet at home. When they were small, I don't think it would have been possible [to be a Supreme Court Justice]. At the present time, because they are now away, either at college or working, I don't have to be home early to tend to their needs." She adds, "It just isn't possible to have a normal family life with this job."

Chapter/Nine

"History will have to determine that."

After more than three years on the Court, Sandra Day O'Connor has had the chance to cast her vote on many cases that affect the lives of Americans. Most observers feel that the newest member of the Supreme Court has joined Justice William Rehnquist and Chief Justice Warren Burger in the conservative wing of the Court. She has agreed with the other justice from her home state so many times that some people call Justice O'Connor and Justice Rehnquist the "Arizona Twins." (Justice Blackmun and Chief Justice Burger, who are both from Minnesota, used to be called the "Minnesota Twins," because of both the baseball team and their similar opinions.) Yet no one considers Justice O'Connor a mere follower. She puts forward her opinions forcefully, and, particularly during her third term on the Court, often argues persuasively for her own interpretation of a case. The *New York Times* said that Justice O'Connor was not just an "ally" of the of the conservative wing of the Court, but a "powerful strategist."

As a conservative, she has consistently defended states' rights. In one case, which involved a state's versus the federal government's jurisdiction over energy laws, Justice O'Connor took a conservative position by voting for the state's right to make its own energy regulations. The Court ruled in that case that Congress could require states to consider plans for electric rates that encourage energy conservation. Justice O'Connor was a member of the minority in that case, and she wrote a dissenting opinion which states that the Court's ruling "permits Congress to kidnap state utility commissions into the national regulatory family." The word "kidnap" is fairly strong, indicating the depth of Justice O'Connor's feelings on the issue of states' rights.

In another case, a prisoner from Ohio was convicted by a state court. However, a federal court ruled that the prisoner should go free because of a mistake the judge in the state court made during the trial. Sandra O'Connor believed that the federal court should not have meddled in the state's case. In her written opinion, she said that such intervention could "seriously undermine the morale of state judges."

According to Justice O'Connor, a states' rights case "as interesting as any the Court might be likely to hear . . . in terms of sheer history and romance" involved a sunken treasure ship. She was referring to the *Nuestra Señora de Atocha*, a Spanish ship that had sunk off the coast of Florida in 1622. It was loaded with gold and other valuables that the Spanish had taken from their New World colonies. After sailing about forty nautical miles it was battered by a hurricane and sunk. All of its treasure, which was intended for King Philip IV of Spain, was lost.

A group of treasure hunters called Treasure Salvors spent years searching the ocean floor and studying ancient Spanish shipping records in an attempt to locate the ship. They were successful in the spring of 1971. Naturally, Treasure Salvors was very excited by its find. They immediately sent deep-sea divers down to explore the wreck. Inside the wreck was a spectacular treasure worth millions of dollars!

However, Treasure Salvors' excitement was dimmed when the state of Florida claimed that it owned the treasure. The basis for the state's claim was a Florida law which said that all "treasure trove, artifacts, and such objects having intrinsic historical and archaeological value which have been abandoned on state-owned lands or state-owned submerged lands shall belong to the state."

So with millions at stake, both sides took their cases to court. At one time, Florida even seized part of the treasure. By the time the case reached the Supreme Court, the issue had broadened. Now the main question being addressed was whether the federal government has the right to seize property owned by a state. In this case the property was the treasure which the state of Florida had taken from the treasure hunters. The case grew even more complicated when the state of Florida and the federal government fell into a dispute over the seaward boundary of Florida. Florida did not fare well; the wreck of the Spanish galleon, according to Florida's new boundaries, was not under the state's jurisdiction. Ten years after finding the treasure, Treasure Salvors won the right to it.

Justice O'Connor agreed with the Court's decision, but she disagreed with some of its reasoning. She is always careful to protect the states from the powerful federal government. Therefore, she disapproved of the federal government stepping into a dispute between a state and one of its citizens.

Several sex discrimination cases have come before the Supreme Court during Sandra O'Connor's service there. In one case, a law firm required women to wait ten years before becoming partners while allowing men to do so after only six years. The attorney for the law firm maintained that the laws against sex discrimination didn't apply to law partnerships. He said that Congress, in writing the law, had intended that those partnerships be exempt. The *New York Times* Court reporter wrote that Justice O'Connor spoke to the attorney "in a tone of strained patience," noting that "Congress well knew how to write exemptions [to the discrimination law] . . . when it wanted to. You are asking us to create [an exemption] ourselves." The Court, and Justice O'Connor, ruled in favor of the woman lawyer. Justice O'Connor also joined the majority in voting that an all-male club, the Jaycees, must admit women. The Jaycees had tried to expel branches of their club in Minneapolis and St. Paul, Minnesota, because they had members of both sexes.

In another case, a young man sued a Mississippi nursing school. The school did not admit male students. The young man wanted to become a nurse. Justice O'Connor voted in favor of the man. Her reasoning was clear: if it is illegal for men to discriminate against women, then it is equally illegal for women to discriminate against men.

However, Justice O'Connor did rule that a federal law forbidding sex discrimination in colleges applies only to those departments receiving aid from the government. In other words, if a college has a big athletic budget for men and a small one for women, no government aid may be given for physical education. Yet government money for scientific research in the same college will not be affected as long as there is no discrimination in that department.

Racial discrimination has also been an issue before the Supreme Court. In one important case, a group of white firefighters was laid off because of budget cuts. Many black firefighters, who had been hired more recently than the white workers, were kept on the job. According to the union contract, the layoffs should have been made according to seniority (time on the job). In a seniority system, the last workers to be hired are the first to be fired. However, since the black workers had all been hired last, layoffs according to the contract would have resulted in an all-white force. Moreover, just a few years back the city had been ordered by a court to hire more blacks in order to achieve a better balance of races. This kind of plan is called "affirmative action," and is in use in many places around the country. Affirmative action plans call for special employment policies (hiring more women or minorities) to make up for discrimination in the past. The Supreme Court majority, which included Justice O'Connor, ruled that the layoffs should have been made according to the contract. In her opinion, Justice O'Connor wrote that a court may not grant special treatment to someone simply because the group they belong to has been badly affected by a seniority system. The Court, said Justice O'Connor, "must balance the interests of all" the people involved.

Perhaps the most controversial issue Sandra O'Connor has had to consider on the Court is abortion. Several abortion cases, considered as a group, came before the Court in 1983 during Justice O'Connor's third term. One was known as *City of Akron* v. *Akron Center for Reproductive Health*. The city government of Akron, Ohio, had passed various laws regulating abortions. According to the Akron laws, abortions performed after the first three months of pregnancy had to take place in a hospital. Also, a pregnant woman was required to wait twenty-four hours before receiving an abortion, and the attending doctor had to make certain statements to a woman before the abortion to ensure that she understood what she was doing. In a similar case, *Planned Parenthood* v. *Ashcroft*, the state of Missouri was requiring that abortions performed after the first three months of pregnancy be done in a hospital. Missouri law also stated that a second doctor had to be present during late abortions in case of emergency, and that a report had to be filed on each abortion performed.

The majority of the Court ruled that the Akron regulations were unconstitutional, and that while Missouri could require the presence of a second doctor, it could not restrict abortions to a hospital after the third month of pregnancy. The majority of the Court also joined in an opinion, written by Associate Justice Lewis Powell, which stated that the original legalization of abortion in 1973 was correct and proper.

Justice O'Connor disagreed with the majority vote. She wrote a twenty-five-page opinion in which she said that the Akron's restrictions on abortion should have been allowed to remain as law. She further stated that the Court should stop relying on three-month, or trimester, intervals of pregnancy in order to formulate laws. According to Justice O'Connor, the state has a fundamental interest in protecting potential human life throughout pregnancy. While she did not state that abortion should be outlawed, Justice O'Connor's opinion was hailed by many anti-abortion groups—the same groups who had so bitterly opposed her nomination in 1981. She was also criticized by those who believe that abortion is a woman's right, including several feminist groups which had been happy about the idea of having a woman on the Supreme Court.

Sandra O'Connor has shown a tough "law-and-order" position in many cases regarding the rights of prisoners. She agreed with the majority of the Court that if the police act in a reasonable manner during an arrest, believing a warrant for an arrest is properly made, the arrest should stand, even if the warrant is later shown to have an error in it. She also ruled that evidence that is obtained illegally should be allowed in a trial if it would have been discovered later in a legal manner. Previously, the rule was that no illegally found evidence could be used. She joined the majority of the Court in stating that cells in a prison may be searched without a warrant, and that prisoners did not have to be present during the search. She also agreed with the Court's decision that a juvenile may be kept in prison before his or her trial if the court feels there is a strong possibility the prisoner will commit more crimes.

During her first week on the Supreme Court, the *New York Times* Court reporter wrote that, "Of the ways in which Sandra Day O'Connor is different from the other justices, her political savvy, relative youth, and continued openness to the world at large are at least as significant as gender. Sex may turn out to be the least important difference of all." In other words, the reporter believed that Justice O'Connor would not bring any special attitudes or influence to the Court simply because she is a woman. Sandra O'Connor tends to agree. She has said that the importance of her presence on the Court is not that she will decide cases as a woman, but that a woman is finally in a position to decide cases. "In terms of it affecting the workings of the Court, or the relationships of the judges with each other," she says, "I don't think [being a woman] has been a factor." However, she adds, "I imagine that my work has been scrutinized [looked at] more closely than perhaps that of some of my colleagues because of the curiosity people have had."

Justice Harry Blackmun once told an interviewer that Sandra O'Connor "brings to the Court a distinct approach to women's issues, and certainly that voice has been lacking for one hundred and ninety years." However, he adds that, "So far as the operation of the Court is concerned, the routine, the day-to-day duties that we all follow, her presence has not made any difference at all. We do things exactly as we did before. The justice is able, articulate. . . . She gives no quarter, she asks no quarter, and she's a fine justice." Justice Blackmun also believes that Sandra O'Connor has changed the decisions of the Court to the same degree that any other new justice changes them—exactly one-ninth, since she holds one out of nine votes.

Certainly, Justice Blackmun has not felt it necessary to treat Justice O'Connor in a special way because she is a woman. The nine judges of the Court work under enormous pressure. They are quite conscious that their decisions are final, and have great power to influence American life. Consequently, the judges often are extremely committed to their own views on a particular issue. In the written opinions the justices may publish after each case, they sometimes criticize their colleagues. Years ago a justice called the members of the Court "nine scorpions in a bottle." Appropriately, the opinions they write may sting another justice. Justice Brennan, for example, once wrote that Justice O'Connor's reasoning in a certain case was "incomprehensible and tortuous." Sandra O'Connor replied in her own opinion that Justice Brennan's ideas were also "incomprehensible." She once called Justice Blackmun's views on a case "an absurdity."

However, none of this harms the justices' relationships with each other. They all understand that the impatience they sometimes show each other is simply the result of pressure and a passionate desire to administer the law correctly. As Justice Blackmun once said, "We all play hardball a little too much, on occasion. But the friendship and the mutual respect, I believe, continues."

Justice O'Connor has enough faith in herself to withstand criticism. She told an interviewer once, "I am not a person who carries a lot of tension around. I try to do the best job I can and then never look back."

Sandra O'Connor notes that more and more women are joining the legal profession. When she graduated from law school in 1952, only 3 percent of new law students were women. As late as 1971, women accounted for less than 1 percent of the lawyers in the federal judiciary system. Now, things are changing. Mrs. O'Connor states that, "There is no doubt with the large number of women who are in law schools today that we are going to see dramatic differences over the next twenty years as the number of women in private practice, the number of women on the bench around the country in state and federal courts, and the number of women who are active in bar associations increases." She adds, "The women we typically see coming in to argue before this Court today are generally of very high caliber. I expect that they will continue to perform very ably as they appear in greater numbers."

Justice O'Connor urges our society to search for other ways to settle disagreements, eliminating some of the pressure on America's overloaded legal system. She also believes that the country should experiment with another high-level court, as Chief Justice Warren Burger has suggested. This "national court of appeals" might take some of the burden of cases away from the Supreme Court.

Sandra Day O'Connor is the Court's youngest justice. Since Supreme Court justices are appointed for life, Justice O'Connor may choose to remain on the

Court for many more years. Her great popularity has made some people wonder whether she might some-day look for a new position—perhaps even run for vice-president. Sandra O'Connor denies that she has further ambitions. "This is it," she says emphatically. When asked about her influence on the country as the first woman on the Supreme Court, Justice O'Connor smiles as she says, "History will have to determine that."

Postscript

From remarks delivered by Justice O'Connor at The Colorado College Commencement on May 31, 1982

During the period when I was making notes in preparation for my remarks today, I received a letter from the parents of a young man of twenty who committed suicide earlier this month while a student at a fine university. His parents had written me and others hoping that their son's death might have meaning if it would cause people such as me to make some helpful suggestions for other young people. They asked me if I saw something which could be said or done to prepare youth for the wide range of pressures and opportunities in the era of history now breaking, to share my views with them and with young people such as you.

No one, of course, has a magic formula to pass on to our youth to prepare them for what those grieving parents described as the "wide range of pressures and opportunities" in our present world. But as I began to think of what I might have learned in the thirty-two years since I sat with my college graduating class, when

I was as you are now—a young person with a degree but little work experience, with high hopes but little actual know-how—[there] come to my mind . . . concepts that may help you as you begin to participate in the mainstream of society.

The first . . . is "creativity." The single most important thing which keeps people vital and interested in the world about them is their creativity. When that is gone, the will to live goes with it. Of all God's gifts to us, the spark of creativity is one of the most important. You have it now, and must never lose it until you draw your last breath. Creativity, as I use the word now, is the spirit of participation in the *resolution* of our problems, both large and small, and the bringing of our own ideas and efforts into the arenas of life . . . .

Sometimes, people in our country, even young, gifted people like you graduates, at some point develop a sense that government and our society have grown so complex and so large that the individual simply cannot impact on the decisions that affect the country and affect all of us. Let me disabuse you [explain the errors] of that notion. My experiences in the executive, legislative, and judicial branches of government and in my position on the Supreme Court all point to this conclusion: an informed, reasoned effort by even *one* citizen can have dramatic impact on how someone, like a legislator, will vote, and what that legislator will then do to impact on how others will vote and act. When I was in the legislature, *one* individual, sometimes with a direct interest in the matter, sometimes without one, could and would, on certain occasions, persuade me by the facts he had mustered, by the clarity of his explanation or by his reasoning, to do something which I never would otherwise have done. I have been at many caucuses when a group of legislators was trying to decide what to do, and, time and time again, my fellow senators would refer to the logic or fairness of what one plain, unknown citizen had said.

I have had an opportunity to view this same basic phenomenon from a different perspective [angle] in my role as a Supreme Court justice. A majority of litigants [people with cases] who come before us are people who are essentially unknown, not only to us but even within their own community. Yet, we resolve their problems and, in so doing, resolve the problems of thousands or millions similarly situated. . . .

The individual can make things happen. It is the individual who can bring a tear to my eye and then cause me to take pen in hand. It is the individual who has acted or tried to act who will not only force a decision but be able to impact on that decision.

So I urge you for the rest of your lives to carry this torch of creativity high in whatever world of influence you live. Not only will our country and our community be beneficiaries of such an effort, but so too will you and those around you.

The second [concept] I urge you to keep before you is . . . "work". Whether your future work is in business, in government, or as a volunteer, try to set your sights on doing something worthwhile and then work hard at it. Theodore Roosevelt said, "Happiness is work at work worth doing," and he was right. I must admit that sometimes when I told our son that I only wanted him to work around the house so it would make him happy, he would inform me that he was happy enough already, and that what our country needed most was conservation of energy, especially his. As I went through life, I did not aspire to become a member of the Supreme Court. What I did was to establish immediate goals and to do every immediate task I had as well as I thought I could do it. Initially, I just tried to be a good lawyer. When I married and had children, I tried to run a good household and home, and to be as good a wife and a mother as I could be. Later, I did my best as a volunteer, as a state senator and as a judge.

I discovered something as I went along. There is a real satisfaction in doing something well, whether it is in a profession, as a volunteer, or at home. Moreover, by doing something as well as you can do it, you are more likely to have new opportunities available to you. People take notice when a job is well done. You will have prepared yourself so that as new pathways open, you can take them. Abraham Lincoln once said: "When I was a young boy, I didn't know what I wanted to do with my life, but I prepared myself for the opportunity that I knew would come my way." That's good advice.

Appendix One
Other Members of the Supreme Court

William Joseph Brennan, Jr.

William Brennan came from an immigrant family that was determined to make a place for itself in American society. His father, who was born in Ireland, worked as a coal carrier in a factory before becoming a union leader and eventually Commissioner of Public Safety in Newark, New Jersey. William, Jr. was born in 1906. He was one of eight children; during his boyhood he earned pocket money delivering milk, pumping gas, and making change for trolley car passengers. A brilliant student, in 1931 William Brennan graduated in the top ten percent of his Harvard Law School class. He worked as a lawyer in Newark, specializing in labor law. During World War II, William Brennan worked for the army and received the Legion of Merit award. In 1949, Mr. Brennan became a judge in New Jersey Superior Court, and in 1952 he joined the supreme court of his home state. During that time Judge Brennan helped design a system of pretrial conferences that streamlined the justice system of New Jersey. In 1956, President Eisenhower appointed him to the Supreme Court of the United States. Justice Brennan normally votes as a liberal in Supreme Court decisions. A liberal, in contrast to a conservative, often assigns greater power to the government.

Byron Raymond White

Justice Byron White has the distinction of being the only Supreme Court justice to be elected to the National Football Hall of Fame! Born in Colorado in 1917, Mr. White excelled as both a scholar and an athlete. He graduated first in his high school class, and earned three varsity letters in football, four in basketball, and three in baseball. In college, he became known as "Whizzer" White and was a star player on the University of Colorado football team. In 1938, he played for the Pittsburgh Steelers, which were then called the Pirates. After one season, he went to Oxford University in England, but returned to the United States when World War II broke out. Then Byron White studied at Yale Law School and played for the Detroit Lions. When the United States entered the war in 1941, Mr. White joined the navy, where he met a young officer named John Fitzgerald Kennedy. After the war he finished his degree at Yale and then clerked for the then-chief justice of the Supreme Court, Frederick Vinson. After several years of private practice, Lawyer White was appointed by President Kennedy to the post of deputy attorney general. In 1962, Kennedy named him to the Supreme Court. Justice White's votes are unpredictably liberal and conservative, depending on the nature of the case.

Thurgood Marshall

The first black justice of the Supreme Court, Thurgood Marshall was famous even before President Lyndon Johnson appointed him to that post. He was born in Baltimore, Maryland in 1908. Thurgood Marshall was the great-grandson of a slave and the son of a teacher and a servant at an all-white yacht club. Mr. Marshall attended Lincoln University in Pennsylvania, and then studied law at Howard University in Washington, D.C. After graduating first in his class, Mr. Marshall joined the National Association for the Advancement of Colored People (NAACP), an organization that strives to achieve equal rights for black people. For over twenty years, Thurgood Marshall worked with the NAACP to help rid the country of prejudice in housing, schools, and government. As a lawyer, Mr. Marshall brought thirty-two civil rights cases before the Supreme Court, and won twenty-nine of them. His most famous case was the historic *Brown v. the Board of Education of Topeka, Kansas*, which was tried in 1954. Lawyer Marshall argued that separate schools for black and white children were unfair, and deprived black children of their right to an equal education. The Supreme Court ruled in his favor. In 1961, President John Kennedy appointed Thurgood Marshall a judge on the Court of Appeals. Four years later Lyndon Johnson appointed him solicitor general of the Justice Department. President Johnson then named him to the Supreme Court in 1967. Justice Marshall is one of the Court's most consistently liberal members.

Warren Earl Burger

The chief justice of the United States was born in St. Paul, Minnesota in 1907. His father was a railroad cargo inspector and salesperson. To help his family, Warren Burger took his first job—delivering newspapers—at the age of nine. A natural at many things, Warren Burger played in his high school band, excelled in sports, served as student council president, and edited the school newspaper. He attended college and law school at night, supporting himself by selling insurance during the day. In 1931, after graduating with honors from law school, Mr. Burger practiced law and taught part time at William Mitchell College of Law. He was also active in state politics, helping to organize Minnesota's Young Republican Club in 1934. In 1953, he moved to Washington, D.C. to become an assistant attorney general. By 1956, Mr. Burger had become a judge on the United States Court of Appeals. In 1969, President Richard Nixon appointed him chief justice of the Supreme Court. A conservative, Chief Justice Burger often votes the same way as William Rehnquist and Sandra Day O'Connor.

Harry Andrew Blackmun

Justice Blackman was born in Illinois in 1908, but he grew up in St. Paul, Minnesota where he was good friends with Warren Burger. An excellent scholar, Harry Blackmun got a scholarship to Harvard University, where he majored in math. To earn pocket money,

Mr. Blackmun worked as a tutor and a janitor while in college. In 1932, he received his law degree and returned to Minnesota, where he clerked for federal judge John Sanborn. He then joined a law firm, and also taught at the St. Paul College of Law and the University of Minnesota Law School. In 1950, Mr. Blackmun became the lawyer for the Mayo Clinic, a famous hospital in Minnesota. In 1959, President Dwight Eisenhower appointed him to the United States Court of Appeals, where he was considered moderately liberal in civil rights cases and moderately conservative in criminal cases. In 1970, after President Richard Nixon's first two appointees to the Supreme Court were rejected by the Senate, Harry Blackmun was named to the post, and was confirmed unanimously. During the first few years of his term, Justice Blackmun and Chief Justice Burger were often called the "Minnesota Twins" because they often voted the same way and came from the same home state.

Lewis Franklin Powell, Jr.

A native of the south, Lewis Powell was born in 1907 in Suffolk, Virginia. He studied at Washington and Lee University in Lexington, Virginia, where he completed the normal, three-year law school course in only two years. Mr. Powell also attended Harvard Law School. After graduation, he joined a Virginia law firm. He was active in community affairs, serving as president of the Virginia state board of education and as president of the Richmond school board. During the tense years of the early civil rights movement, there was a great deal of pressure put on Mr. Powell to close the schools rather than to allow black and white children in the same class. However, Mr. Powell managed to keep all the schools open. In 1964, Lewis Powell became president of the American Bar Association, an organization of lawyers, and in 1968 he became president of the American College of Trial Lawyers. He has also served as vice-president of the National Legal Aid and Defender Association, a group that supports better legal services for poor people. President Richard Nixon nominated Justice Powell to the Supreme Court in 1971. Justice Powell has been called "the great balancer" of the Court, maintaining a central position between the liberals and the conservatives.

William Hubbs Rehnquist

William Rehnquist was known as the "brains of the Justice Department" before Richard Nixon appointed him to the Supreme Court in 1972. Born in Milwaukee, Wisconsin, in 1924, Mr. Rehnquist served in the Air Force during World War II. After the war, Mr. Rehnquist studied at Stanford and Harvard universities. He graduated first in his class at Stanford Law School, the same class that included his future colleague, Sandra Day O'Connor. After graduation, Mr. Rehnquist clerked for Justice Robert Jackson of the Supreme Court for a year and a half, and then went into private practice in Phoenix, Arizona. President Richard Nixon chose William Rehnquist for a post in the Justice

Department in 1969, and eventually nominated him to replace Justice John Harlan on the nation's highest court in 1971. Justice Rehnquist is a conservative who often votes the same way as Justice O'Connor.

John Paul Stevens

Justice Stevens also began his law career as a clerk for the Supreme Court. He was born in 1920 in Chicago, Illinois to a wealthy family. Although the Stevens family lost a great deal of money in the Crash of 1929, they were still able to provide John Paul with a comfortable childhood during the Depression. Mr. Stevens graduated with honors from the University of Chicago in 1941. During World War II, he was an intelligence officer for the navy and worked at breaking secret codes. After the war, Mr. Stevens attended Northwestern University School of Law, where he graduated first in his class. He went to the Supreme Court as clerk to Justice Wiley Rutledge in 1947, and later joined a Chicago law firm. He also taught part time at the University of Chicago and Northwestern law schools. In 1970, President Richard Nixon appointed him to the federal Court of Appeals. In 1975, President Gerald Ford named him to the highest court. Justice Stevens is often called a "judge's judge," because of his scholarly, well-written opinions.

Appendix Two

Famous Supreme Court Cases

Note: Cases are named by listing the two opponents in court. If Mr. Smith sues Mr. Jones, the case is called *Smith* v. *Jones*. "V." is an abbreviation of the Latin word *versus*, which means "against."

Cases are listed in the order in which they happened. Notice that the Court often changed its mind, as the times or beliefs of the American people demanded.

Marbury **v.** *Madison* (1803): In this historic decision, the Supreme Court declared that it had the right to review laws passed by Congress and to declare them constitutional or unconstitutional: that is, whether or not they are in line with the ideas expressed in the United States Constitution. A constitutional law is allowed to stand. An unconstitutional law must be taken off the books.

Martin **v.** *Hunter's Lesee* (1816): The Supreme Court has the power to review and possibly change the decisions of a state court.

Gibbons **v.** *Ogden* (1824): The Constitution gives Congress the power to regulate commerce between states. The Court ruled that "commerce" includes all businesses as well as transportation.

Worcester v. Georgia (1832): The federal government in Washington has power over Indian (Native American) affairs; state governments may not make laws affecting Indian territories.

Scott v. Sanford (1857): The famous "Dred Scott" case. The Court ruled that Congress did not have the authority to forbid slavery in American territories.

Texas v. White (1869): The Court ruled that since states may not secede (leave) the union, the southern states who fought the North in the Civil War had never really left the United States.

Bradwell v. the State of Illinois (1873): The Court ruled that women may be forbidden a license to practice law.

Yick Wo v. Hopkins (1886): All persons, regardless of race, color, or nationality, are entitled to equal protection under the law.

Plessy v. Ferguson (1896): The Court allowed a state law requiring trains to have separate sections for black and white people to stand. The Court said that "separate but equal" facilities were constitutional. This decision was overturned in 1954, in the *Brown* v. *The Board of Education* case.

Holden v. Hardy (1898): The Court approved a Utah law that limited the number of hours miners could work underground, and said that states may make laws to protect workers' health.

Georgia v. Tennessee (1907): A state may sue another state in a federal court to stop the other state from polluting its air.

Buchanan v. Warley (1917): Cities may not make laws

forbidding blacks in some neighborhoods and whites in others.

Schenck v. United States (1919): While freedom of speech and freedom of the press are guaranteed by the Constitution, words that create "a clear and present danger" may not be used. For example, a person may not scream, "Fire!" in a crowded movie theater when there is no fire.

Whitney v. California (1927): Laws that make it a crime to join or form a group that wants to overthrow the government are constitutional.

Nebbia v. New York (1934): States may regulate businesses for the public good, as long as the regulations are reasonable.

Schechter Poultry Corporation v. United States (1935): The National Industrial Recovery Act, a law that was passed to help lift the country out of the Great Depression, was ruled unconstitutional because it gave too much power to the president.

Brown v. Mississippi (1936): Confessions obtained by force may not be used in a trial.

West Coast Hotel Company v. Parrish (1937): Laws setting the lowest salaries (minimum wages) for certain types of work are constitutional.

Johnson v. Zerbst (1938): All prisoners have the right to a lawyer during their trial if they wish.

Chaplinsky v. New Hampshire (1942): Freedom of speech is guaranteed by the Constitution, but a state may make it a crime to curse or use "fighting words" in public.

West Virginia State Board of Education v. Barnette (1943): Students have the right to remain silent and may not be forced to say the Pledge of Allegiance in school.

Brown v. the Board of Education of Topeka, Kansas (1954): Separate schools for children of different races can never be really equal, and are therefore illegal. This ruling overturned the *Plessy* v. *Ferguson* decision of 1896.

Mapp v. Ohio (1961): Illegally obtained evidence may not be used in a trial.

Engel v. Vitale (1962): Public school officials may not require students to recite a prayer, even if that prayer does not refer to any specific religion.

Miranda v. Arizona (1966): When people are arrested, they must be told their rights before they are questioned. These rights include the right to remain silent and the right to have a lawyer. The prisoners must also be told that anything they say may be used against them in a trial.

Jones v. Alfred H. Mayer Co. (1968): It is illegal to discriminate against people because of race in the sale or rental of houses and apartments, even when the owner is a private citizen. It had long been illegal for the government to discriminate against people by race. This decision outlawed discrimination by ordinary people as well.

Swann v. Charlotte-Mecklenburg County Board of Education (1971): In order to do away with segregated schools (schools that are only for black or white students) children may be bused to schools in other neighborhoods. School district lines may also be redrawn to group blacks and whites in the same schools.

Lemon v. Kurtzman (1971): The United States Constitution does not allow the government to become involved with religion. However, the government may aid religious schools if the purpose of that aid is not religious and does not cause the government to become "entangled" with religion. Therefore, the government may give money to school lunch programs in religious schools, but it may not pay for religious books or bibles.

Furman v. Georgia (1972): All the death penalty laws in the United States were declared unconstitutional by this decision.

Branzburg v. Hayes (1972): Freedom of the press is guaranteed by the Constitution. However, this guarantee does not allow reporters to refuse to give information concerning a crime to a grand jury.

Roe v. Wade (1973): No state may make a law forbidding abortion, except during the last three months before birth.

Miller v. California (1973): State governments may regulate or ban magazines, books, and movies that deal with sex if the content would probably offend the average person in the community, and if the material has no scientific or artistic value.

United States v. Nixon (1974): The president of the United States may be ordered to turn over evidence in a criminal trial. This is the famous "Watergate" case. President Richard Nixon had to turn over tapes of his private conversations because of this decision.

Gregg v. Georgia (1976): Death penalties are allowed if the judge or jury considers the circumstances of each crime. This decision overrules the *Furman* v. *Georgia* case of 1972.

Regents of University of California v. Bakke (1978): A state medical school may not set aside a certain number of places for non-white students. The Court said that race may be one of many things considered by the college, but not the only thing.

Orr v. Orr (1979): It is illegal to allow women to receive alimony payments after a divorce while denying the same right to men.

United Steelworkers of America v. Weber (1979): Employers may not hire or fire employees simply because of their race. However, employers may set up special programs aimed at employing members of minority groups that have been discriminated against in the past.

Harris v. MacRae (1980): Congress passed a law saying that money from the American government may not be used for abortions unless the life of the mother is in danger or in certain other circumstances. The Court ruled that this law is constitutional.

Rostker v. Goldberg (1981): The law that allows men but not women to be drafted is constitutional.

Edwards v. Arizona (1981): If a prisoner asks for a lawyer, the police may not question him or her again until the lawyer arrives, unless the prisoner chooses to speak.

Grover City College v. Bell (1984): Federal law forbidding sex discrimination in schools applies only to those departments receiving federal money.

Firefighters v. Stotts (1984): A court may not order an employer to protect black jobs at the expense of a seniority system.

Bibliography

"And Now, the Arizona Twins." *Time* (April 19, 1982): p. 49.

Arizona Republic, numerous articles, 1981-1982.

"As Justice O'Connor Opens Her Books." *US News* (September 14, 1981): p. 13.

Feigen, B. "Sandra Day O'Connor, Will She Make a Difference?" *Vogue* (November, 1981): p. 118.

"First Woman Justice—Impact on the Supreme Court." *US News* (July 20, 1981): p. 20.

Footlick, J. and D. Friendly. "A Woman for the Court." *Newsweek* (July 20, 1981): p. 16.

Frank, John. unpublished letter.

Goldwater, Barry. unpublished letter.

Hait, Pam. "Sandra Day O'Connor, Warm, Witty and Wise." *McCalls* (April, 1982): p. 40.

Hecht, L. and C. Chafran. "Sandra Day O'Connor and the Supremes." *Ms* (October, 1981): p. 71.

Jenkins, John A. "A Candid Talk With Justice Blackmun." *New York Times Magazine* (February 20, 1983): p. 20.

"A Justice Speaks Out." *Cable News Network Interview* (Broadcast November 25, 1982.)

"A Lady Justice, Says Laurence Tribe, Can Bring Cohehesion to a Court that Badly Needs It." *People* (July 20, 1981): p. 31.

Levinson, S. "Should Supreme Court Nominees Have Opinions?" *Nation* (October 17, 1981): p. 375.

Lewis, N. "Justice O'Connor's First Six Months." *New Republic* (March 10, 1982): p. 17.

Mackintosh, P. "Sandra Day O'Connor, First Woman on Our Highest Court." *McCalls* (October, 1982): p. 12.

Magnuson, E. "The Brethren's First Sister." *Time* (July 20, 1981): p. 8

New York Times, numerous articles from July, 1981 to July, 1983.

Newsday, several articles from July, 1981 to July, 1982.

O'Connor, John Jay. unpublished letter.

O'Connor, Sandra Day. interview.

O'Connor, Sandra Day. "A Day in the Life of a Supreme Court Justice." unpublished monograph.

"O'Connor Captures Washington's Heart." *US News* (July 27, 1981): p. 6.

Phoenix Gazette, numerous articles, 1981 to 1982.

Press, A. and D. Camper, "O'Connor's Senate Trial." *Newsweek* (September 21, 1981): p. 73.

"The Private World O'Connor is Joining." *US News* (October 5, 1981): p. 10.

"Reagan's Lady Makes Her Debut." *Newsweek* (July 27, 1981): p. 24.

"Sandra Day O'Connor." *Current Biography* (January, 1982): p. 26.

"Sandra Day O'Connor." *Vogue* (September, 1981): p. 532.

Slip Opinions of Supreme Court Decisions, 1981-1984.

Warner, Carolyn. unpublished letter.

"When a Woman Justice Took the Witness Chair." *US News* (September 21, 1981): p. 13.

Index

abortion, 100-101
American Bar Association, 68
Arizona Court of Appeals, 14,
48-51, 64
Arizona Republican party, 23
Arizona State-County Municipal Affairs Committee,
35-36
"Arizona Twins," 95
Austin High School, 15

Babbit, Governor Bruce, 48
Baker, James, 57
Baker, Senator Howard, 61
Barr, Senator Burton, 41
Blackmun, Justice Harry, 95,
102-103
Bradwell v *Illinois*, 4
Brandeis, Justice Louis, 5
Brennan, Justice William, 103
Burger, Chief Justice Warren,
71-72, 88, 95, 104
Burgess, Senator Isabel A., 34
Bush, Vice-President George,
69

Christian Science Monitor, 68

City of Akron v *Akron Center
for Reproductive Health*,
100-101
Day, Ada Mae (mother), 8-9,
11, 13, 61
Day, Alan (brother), 13
Day, Ann (sister), 13
Day, Harry (father), 8-13, 16,
61
Deaver, Michael, 57
Denton, Senator Jeremiah, 67

Equal Rights Amendment, 36,
52

Gibson, Dunn and Crutcher
(law firm), 19-20
Goldwater, Senator Barry, 53,
63, 65, 69

Heard Museum, 39

Jackson, President Andrew, 5
Jacquin, Senator William, 35,
65
Jaycees, 98
Johnson, President Lyndon, 5

Kennedy, Senator Edward, 61
Kirkpatrick, Ambassador
    Jeane, 52

Lazy B (ranch), 8-10, 13, 15,
    17-18, 61, 66

Manzo, Flournoy (cousin),
    11-13
Maricopa Board of Adjust
    ments and Appeals, 23
Maricopa County Superior
    Court, 43
Marshall, Justice Thurgood,
    5, 75
Medicaid, 37
Meese, Edwin, 57
"Minnesota Twins," 95
Miller and Chevalier (law
    firm), 70
Myers, Charles, 53

National Organization of
    Women, 61
National Women's Political
    Caucus, 61
New York Times, 95, 102
Nixon, President Richard M.,
    40
Nuestra Senora de Atocha,
    96

O'Connor, John Jay III, 17-
    18, 21-22, 55, 61, 66, 70-72

O'Connor, Justice Sandra
Day:
    abortion cases and, 62-
        64, 67
    ancestors of, 7, 11
    as appellate judge, 14,
        48-51
    as assistant attorney gen-
        eral, 25
    as attorney in Germany,
        21
    childhood of, 9-13
    children of, 22-23, 39, 47,
        61, 94
    in college, 16-17
    confirmation hearing of,
        15, 41, 66-69
    as county deputy attor-
        ney, 20
    ERA and, 36
    in elementary school, 13-
        15
    financial statement of, 44,
        66
    in high school, 15-16
    law practice of, 20-23
    in law school, 17-18
    as senate majority leader,
        37, 40-41
    marriage of, 18
    nomination to Supreme
        Court of, 59-61
    prisoners' rights cases
        and, 101-102

O'Connor, Justice Sandra Day, continued:
  racial discrimination cases and, 99-101
  sex discrimination cases and, 98-99
  as state senator, 34-41
  states' rights cases and, 96-98
  as Supreme Court justice, 84-86, 91, 93
  swearing in of, 5, 71
  as trial judge, 43-48
  volunteer activities of, 23-24, 39, 47
  voting record of (as justice), 96-102
  women's rights and, 20, 22-23, 36, 67-68
O'Neill, Senator Thomas "Tip," 65

Paradise Valley, 20, 24, 55, 66
Planned Parenthood v *Ashcroft*, 100
Powell, Justice Lewis, 101

Radford School, 13
Reagan, President Ronald, 5, 20, 51-55, 57-62, 69, 71
Rehnquist, Justice William, 18, 53, 86, 88, 91, 95
right-to-life movement, 62-64, 68, 101

Smith, Atty. General William French, 20, 53, 55, 57, 69
Stanford Law Review, 17-18
Stanford Law School, 17-18, 53, 67
Stanford University, 16-17
Stevens, Justice John Paul, 86
Stewart, Justice Potter, 51, 71

Taney, Justice Roger, 5
Thurmond, Senator Strom, 61, 67, 69

United States Supreme Court:
  ceremonies of, 75, 87-93
  interior of building, 87-89
  law clerks and, 86
  schedule of, 84-85
  voting procedures of, 85, 90, 92-93

Washington, President George, 5
White, Justice Byron, 75, 86
William and Mary Law Review, 54
Williams, Governor Jack, 34
Wilson, President Woodrow, 5

About the Authors

Harold and Geraldine Woods are the authors of thirty books for young people and adults. In addition to their writing careers, the Woods teach English and Reading in two private schools in New York City.

The Woods originally became interested in Sandra Day O'Connor because of her position as first woman on the Supreme Court. They believe that traditional ideas of men's and women's roles are now changing, and that women who are moving into positions of power are actually pioneers. The authors felt it would be interesting to readers to find out how one such "pioneer" achieved her position, and how her new role affected her life.